CULTURES OF THE WORLD®

ALGERIA

Falaq Kagda & Zawiah Abdul Latif

Marshall Cavendish
Benchmark

New York

PICTURE CREDITS
Cover photo: © Norbert Eisele-Hein / Visum / The Image Works
alt.TYPE / Reuters: 4, 32, 38, 84 • Anaik Frantz / Seuil: 111 • Andes Press Agency: 81 • Audrius Tomonis: 135 • Bes Stock: 1, 5, 11, 35, 42, 45, 50, 68, 95, 105, 118, 124 • Björn Klingwall: 47, 70, 74, 87, 94 • C. Laoussati: 21, 115 • Corbis: 96 • Farid Zadi and Ji-Young Park: 130, 131 • Focus Team–Italy: 60, 91, 97, 98, 128 • Getty Images: 77, 114 • HBL Network Photo Agency: 3, 18, 40, 58, 83, 85, 89, 103, 104 • Hulton Getty: 28, 31, 72, 109 • Hutchison Library: 8, 16, 20, 43, 62, 66, 76, 78, 99, 116 • Image Bank: 12, 14, 59, 120 • North Wind Picture Archives: 61, 93 • Parrot Pascal / Corbis Sygma: 121 • Photolibrary / Alamy: 6, 24, 33 • Photolibrary: 46, 55 • Rabah Seffal: 36, 63, 64, 69, 80, 101, 107, 119, 123, 126 • Victor Englebert: 65

PRECEDING PAGE
Rural Algerian boys at a cattle market in Algeria's desert.

Publisher (U.S.): Michelle Bisson
Editors: Deborah Grahame, Mabelle Yeo
Copyreader: Sherry Chiger
Designer: Jailani Basari
Cover picture researcher: Connie Gardner
Picture researcher: Thomas Khoo

Marshall Cavendish Benchmark
99 White Plains Road
Tarrytown, NY 10591
Web site: www.marshallcavendish.us

© Times Editions Private Limited 1997
© Marshall Cavendish International (Asia) Private Limited 2009
All rights reserved. First edition 1997. Second edition 2009.
® "Cultures of the World" is a registered trademark of Times Publishing Limited.

Originated and designed by Times Editions Private Limited
An imprint of Marshall Cavendish International (Asia) Private Limited
A member of Times Publishing Limited

All Internet sites were correct and accurate at the time of printing. All monetary figures in this publication are in U.S. dollars.

Library of Congress Cataloging-in-Publication Data
Kagda, Falaq.
    Algeria / by Falaq Kagda & Zawiah Abdul Latif. — 2nd ed.
      p. cm. — (Cultures of the world)
    Summary: "Provides comprehensive information on the geography, history, wildlife, governmental structure, economy, cultural
        diversity, peoples, religion, and culture of Algeria"—Provided by publisher.
    Includes bibliographical references and index.
      ISBN 978-0-7614-2085-9
    1. Algeria—Juvenile literature. I. Latif, Zawiah Abdul. II. Title.
DT275.K34 2007
965—dc22   2007014888

Printed in China

9 8 7 6 5 4 3 2 1

CONTENTS

Algerian schoolchildren
in the midst of a lesson
at school.

Farm laborers sorting through harvested olives in the village of Tazmelt. Olive oil production has been one of the mainstays of the Algerian economy for the past century but is on the decline due to increasing occurrences of drought.

INTRODUCTION

ALGERIA FORMS PART OF the region that its early Arab conquerors called Jazirat al Maghrib, or "Island of the West"—the land between the "Sea of Sand" (the Sahara) and the Mediterranean Sea. Similar to those of other North African countries, Algeria's population is divided between the original Berber inhabitants and the Arab conquerors who settled there in the seventh century. Colonized later by the Turks, and then the French, Algeria finally gained independence on July 5, 1962. But in late 1991 it fell into the grip of a civil war that lasted 11 years.

Under current president Abdelaziz Bouteflika, Algeria entered the 21st century in relative peace. It is also secure in its significant role in the world hydrocarbons economy and in its elected multiparty government. Algeria has seen some measure of success in reconciling its culturally diverse population by recognizing aspects of Islam—a religion shared by a great majority of Algerians—and Arab and Berber ethnic identity as essential elements of its shared national identity. Although the specter of high unemployment and the continuing small-scale activities of extremist militants still lurk in the background, this vast country's comprehensive structural reforms could potentially tackle these social and economic tribulations.

GEOGRAPHY

THE DEMOCRATIC REPUBLIC OF ALGERIA, in northwest Africa, is part of the Maghrib, a region in North Africa between the Mediterranean Sea and the Sahara. The Maghrib includes the Atlas Mountains and the coastal plain of northwest Africa. The name *Maghrib*—Arabic for "west"— geopolitically refers to Morocco, Algeria, Tunisia, Libya, Western Sahara, and sometimes Mauritania. Spain was included at the time of Moorish domination (eighth to 15th centuries).

The word *Algeria* stems from the name of the city of Algiers, and both names come from the Arabic word *al-jaza'ir*. This Arabic word originally referred to the cluster of islands off the coast of Algiers, which only became part of the mainland in 1525.

Algeria is Africa's second largest country, after Sudan. Algeria is bordered by Tunisia in the northeast, Libya to the east, Niger and Mali to the south, and Mauritania, Morocco, and Western Sahara to the west and northwest. The Mediterranean Sea defines Algeria's northern border. Algeria's geographical position at the crossroads of Europe, Africa, and the Middle East has given it a prominent position in world affairs.

TOPOGRAPHY

Topographically Algeria consists of a series of contrasting, approximately parallel east-west zones. The narrow alluvial plains along the coast—the most fertile land in Algeria—are separated from the Sahara by the ranges and plateaus of the Atlas Mountains. The Tell Atlas mountain range is more than 932 miles (1,500 m) in length, and its highest summit is 7,572 feet (2,308 m) above sea level. The Tell Atlas includes the Hodna range and the spectacular Djurdjura Massif of Kabylia in northeastern Algeria.

Opposite: **Modern buildings dot the city landscape of Algiers, with the monument of independence looming in the background.**

The desert has a variety of features and looks, such as the lunarlike landscape of the Tassili Plateau.

A semiarid plateau with an average elevation of 3,500 feet (1,070 m) separates the Tell Atlas from the Saharan Atlas. In the east, the plateau merges with the Aurès Mountains, which boast Mount Chelia, the highest peak in northern Algeria at 7,638 feet (2,328 m). South of the Saharan Atlas is the immense Sahara Desert, with its gravel expanses; plateaus; *ergs* (ehrgs), or sand dunes; and the fascinating lunarlike Ahaggar Massif, where Mount Tahat, the nation's highest peak, rises to 9,852 feet (3,003 m).

THE TELL REGION Most Algerian cities and 90 percent of the population inhabit the fertile coastal area called the Tell, which means "hill" in Arabic. The Tell, the country's best farmland, was named for its rolling hills and valleys. Most of Algeria's rivers are found here, and they help to keep the land fertile. Two of the best areas for agriculture are the Mitidja Plain and the Bejaïa Plain. The rivers flood during the rainy season and drain into the Mediterranean. In the summer they often slow to a trickle, and dry riverbeds are a common sight.

THE HIGH PLATEAU REGION Separating the Tell and the Saharan Mountains, this rocky and dry region rises 1,300–4,300 feet (400–1,300 m) above sea level. Cattle, sheep, and goats graze on small clumps of vegetation, shrubs, scrub pines, oak trees, and wild esparto grass (needlegrass) dotting the plateau and grassland leading into the Saharan Atlas Mountains. Only about 3 million Algerians, mostly herders, live there. Some are nomads who roam from pasture to pasture to feed their flocks on the grasses and shrubs that cover most of the area.

For three to five weeks each summer, the sirocco sweeps the plateaus. This powerful, dusty, hot wind whips northward from the Sahara, blowing sand as far as the coastal Tell.

CLIMATE AND DRAINAGE

Algerian weather varies according to its geography. In the Tell, the Mediterranean keeps the climate mild, with temperatures averaging between 70°F (21°C) and 75°F (24°C) in summer and 52°F (11°C) in winter. Rainfall is abundant along the coast, ranging from 16 to 26 inches (40 cm–67 cm) annually, although less rain falls in the west (15 inches, or 38 cm, annually in Oran) than in the east (26 inches, or 66 cm, annually in Algiers). The Tell Atlas is also much drier in the west than it is in Kabylia in the east, which receives only about 16–32 inches (40–80 cm) of rainfall a year. Snow on the Djurdjura Massif also supplies water when it melts in spring. The only significant stream, Cheliff in the coastal plain, is impassable but provides water for irrigation and hydroelectric power.

In the ranges and plateaus of the Atlas Mountains, temperatures are harsher, ranging from 39°F (4°C) to 82°F (28°C). Rainfall is limited in the High Plateau region, but during the rainy season streams drain into the shallow salt marshes called *shatts* (sh-UTS).

In the desert, underground rivers offer the only water. Most of the practically rainless Sahara receives less than 5 inches (13 cm) of rainfall a year. A small part of the desert crosses the Tropic of Cancer, where temperatures are blistering even in winter. Daytime temperatures have climbed to an unforgiving 122°F (50°C) in the midday sun. However, the dryness allows the air to cool quickly once the sun disappears.

Since 1975 the Algerian government has tried to curb the encroaching desert. The grandest project was the barrage vert *(BAH-rahge vair), or "green barrier." Rows of Aleppo pine trees have been planted along the Saharan Atlas ridge from Morocco to the Tunisian border. Unfortunately the project was aborted in the early 1980s, as the desert crept northward more quickly than workers could plant trees.*

THE WORLD'S LARGEST DESERT

The Sahara is the largest nonpolar (hot) desert in the world. Spanning the continent from the Atlantic Ocean to the Red Sea, it extends north from the Niger River and Lake Chad to the Atlas Mountains and the Mediterranean Sea. The name *Sahara* is derived from the Arabic word for "desert." The grasslands of West Africa, which form the Sahara's southern boundary, are called the Sahel. The name is derived from Arabic word *sahil*, which means "coast." The idea is that the Sahel is the coast to the great "sea" of the Sahara. This also explains why the camel is often referred to as the "ship of the desert." The Sahara covers about 3,500,000 square miles (9,060,000 square km). Morocco, Algeria, Tunisia, Mali, Niger, Chad, and Sudan have large desert regions. Most of Libya, Egypt, and Mauritania are located in the Sahara.

The folded rocks of the Saharan Atlas Mountains delineate the northern boundary of the Algerian Sahara. These mountains once supported extensive Atlas cedar forests, but most trees were harvested for fuel and building supplies. Now the denuded mountains serve mainly as a gateway to the world's largest desert. To the south, the Sahara dashes the image many have of deserts as simply an endless expanse of golden sand. The sand gives way to plateaus of black pebbles. These in turn give way to wide expanses of red sand. Farther southeast are large sandstone rock formations, which signal the beginning of the Ahaggar Mountains. Here towers Mount Tahat, sometimes with snow on its peak.

Oases are the only areas of greenery in the Sahara, and they look unusually built up in the midst of the arid desert. About 1.5 million Algerians, mostly nomads and bedouin, live in the desert. Most settle on oases and survive by growing dates and citrus fruits. Some nomads can be found traveling from pasture to pasture with their camels and other livestock. As major oil fields are located in the northeastern Sahara, one can find derricks and rigs pumping out the oil and natural gas that lie beneath the desert.

The northern Sahara gets about 4–8 inches (10–20 cm) of rainfall a year in winter. During summer, when wet monsoon winds from the Gulf of Guinea penetrate inland to the Sahel, the northern Sahara can receive about 10–20 inches (25–50 cm) of annual rainfall. Most of the Sahara, however, receives less than 5 inches (13 cm) of rainfall annually, and large areas are known to experience no rainfall for years at a time. Thus, rainfall is distributed unevenly, with huge irregularities.

The Sahara experiences average temperature ranges from 14°F to 93°F (-10°C to 34°C), though it can reach a high of 120°F (49°C). There are daily fluctuations of more than 80°F (44°C). When temperatures soar and skies are clear, humidity can go down to a low of 25 percent, the lowest in the world. However, the Sahara's relative humidity is often 4–5 percent. Parts of the Sahara experience 50–75 days per year of wind and blowing sand. Although the climate has remained relatively uniform, extended periods of drought are common. The Sahel has persistently been hit by droughts in the 1960s, the mid-1980s, and the early 1990s.

The Sahara has an extensive network of dry streambeds, or wadis, that were formed during earlier wet periods. Many streams appear in the wadis after rainfall, flowing from the Atlas Mountains and the central Saharan uplands into surrounding basins, where occasional salt marshes, called *sebkhas* (SUB-kahs), are found. Underground sources of water that can support irrigated agriculture are found in many wadis and depressions.

The sands of the Sahara hide a wealth of mineral resources. The desert has substantial crude petroleum reserves. Libya and Algeria are the largest oil producers, and Algeria is also an important producer and exporter of natural gas. In addition, Algeria has iron ore deposits and manganese, and numerous metals are found in the central Saharan uplands.

Truck convoys have mostly replaced the traditional camel caravans that used to traverse the deserts—an image popularized by movies such as *Lawrence of Arabia*. The Saharan road system is steadily expanding. Algeria completed its most extensive trans-Saharan highway project in 1985. The highway crosses the desert from central Algeria to Niger and southern Mali. So far only Algeria and Libya have roads spanning the Sahara. The best road and rail transportation is associated with mineral exploitation. Many international air routes cross the Sahara.

BARBARY APE

The Barbary ape, so called since ancient times, is actually a monkey, not an ape. It is a macaque, *Macaca sylvanus*. The Barbary ape is 15–30 inches (38–76 cm) tall and weighs up to 28 pounds (13 kg). It reaches maturity at three to four years of age and may live for 20 years or more. With thick yellowish brown to black fur and hairless, whitish pink faces, Barbary apes are the only wild monkeys now living in Europe. They occupy caves on the Rock of Gibraltar as well as in the rocky areas of Morocco and Algeria. It is thought that Arabs may have taken them westward during the Arab expansion of the Middle Ages. According to legend, British dominion will end when the Barbary ape, a symbol of British sovereignty, is gone from the British-held Rock of Gibraltar.

Evening temperatures can drop quickly and seem freezing after the scorching daytime heat. Extreme daily temperature variations are common when the harsh sirocco winds blow in from the desert.

FLORA AND FAUNA

Although once quite densely foliated for a country that is more than 80 percent desert, Algeria today is much denuded of its greenery. In the Tell, just west of Algiers, lie citrus groves and vineyards. Fig trees and indigenous olive trees flourish along the coast. Aleppo pine, juniper, and cork trees grow on the rugged mountain slopes of the Kabylia and Aurès along the eastern coast and the southern part of the region.

Vegetation in the semiarid areas includes drinn and esparto grass. Few areas of the desert are completely lacking in vegetation. A minimal cover of xerophytic shrubs (shrubs adapted to hot, dry climates) extends to the northern edge of the desert, coarse grass grows in depressions, and acacia trees and date palms grow in valleys and oases. Thorn woodlands and wooded grasslands are found in the Sahel.

Wildlife is varied, but many species exist in small numbers. Camels are a common sight, and there are other mammals such as boars, antelopes, jackals, hares, and birds such as eagles and vultures. Several endangered Barbary species, which include apes, red deers, hyenas, and leopards, can also be found in Algeria. Some animal life exists even in the desert's interior: poisonous and nonpoisonous snakes, scorpions, insects, small rodents, and on the plateaus, gazelles.

ALGIERS

Algiers is Algeria's oldest, largest, and most historic city. The Phoenicians settled there approximately 3,000 years ago. For almost 500 years Algiers was a colonial capital under Turkish and French rule before becoming the national capital after independence. With a population of more than 3.5 million in 2005, Algiers (in French, Alger) is Algeria's largest city and chief port. *Algiers* and *Algeria* are both derived from the Arabic word *al-jaza'ir*.

Algiers was known to the Romans as Icosium. After it was razed several times by invaders, the Berber-speaking peoples settled in the present site in the 10th century. In 1516 Algiers came under Ottoman influence. Until June 1830, Algiers served as base for corsairs, or pirates, who undertook raids in the Mediterranean and southern Europe and who came to be known in the West as Barbary pirates. The French invaded the city in 1830, and it became the colonial headquarters of France until Algeria's independence in 1962. During World War II, Algiers served as a major headquarters for the Allies, and for a brief period it was the provisional capital of free France.

Algiers is built on a hillside, where European-style buildings surround an old Muslim town overlooking Mediterranean waters. To the west, the Sahel Hills cut off Algiers from surrounding farmlands. Flowers and palm trees line the main road leading to the city center, where a memorial to African culture stands. History lives on in the Prehistory and Ethnographic Museum, which was once the Turkish Bardo Palace. Historic

THE CAMEL

Domesticated thousands of years ago by frankincense traders, who trained the gangly cud chewer to make the long and arduous journey from southern Arabia to the northern regions of the Middle East, the camel went on to become the bedouin's, or desert dweller's, primary source of transport, shade, milk, meat, wool, and hide. But in technologically advanced Saudi Arabia, even the bedouin are not as dependent on the camel as they once were. These days camels are valued more as thoroughbred racing animals and sentimental images of the past than as the mainstay of transportation. But in many parts of Africa and Asia, camels still pull plows, turn waterwheels, and transport people and goods to market along desert routes impassable by wheeled vehicles. The following is an introduction to this amazing creature:

• *ATA ALLAH* ("God's gift") The bedouin name for *Camelus dromedarius*, the one-hump dromedary, also known as the Arabian camel.

• **BEHAVIOR** Unpredictable at best, camels have the reputation of being bad-tempered and obstinate creatures that spit and kick. In reality, they tend to be good-tempered, patient, and intelligent. The moaning and bawling sounds they make when they are loaded up and rising to their feet is like the grunting and heavy breathing of a weight lifter in action, not a sign of displeasure at having to do some work.

• **BODY TEMPERATURE** Camels do not pant, and they sweat minimally. Humans perspire when the outside temperature rises above the normal body temperature of 98.6°F (37°C), but the camel has a unique body thermostat. It can raise its body temperature tolerance level as much as 8°F (4°C) before perspiring, thereby conserving body fluids and avoiding unnecessary water loss. No other mammal can do this. Because the camel's body temperature is often lower than air temperature, a group of resting camels will avoid excessive heat by pressing against each other.

• **EARS** A camel's hearing is acute—even if it chooses to pay no attention when given a command! A camel's ears are lined with fur to filter out sand and dust blowing into the ear canal.

• **EYES** A camel's eyes are large, with a soft, doelike expression. They are protected by a double row of long curly eyelashes that also help keep out sand and dust, while thick bushy eyebrows shield their eyes from the desert sun.

• **FEET** Camels have two toes on each foot with broad, flat, leathery pads underneath. When the camel places its foot down, the pads spread, preventing the foot from sinking into the sand.

When walking, the camel moves both feet on one side of its body, then both feet on the other. This gait suggests the rolling motion of a boat, another explanation for the camel's "ship of the desert" nickname.

• **FOOD** A camel can go for five to seven days with little or no food and water, and it can lose a quarter of its body weight without impairing its normal functions. Domesticated camels rely on man for their preferred diet of dates, grass, and grains such as wheat and oats, but they can also survive on thorny scrub or whatever else they can find—bones, seeds, dried leaves, even their owner's tent.

• **HAIR** Camels come in every shade of brown, from cream to almost black. All camels molt in spring and grow a new coat by autumn. Camel hair is sought after worldwide for high-quality coats, other garments, and artists' brushes, as well as to make traditional bedouin rugs and tents. A camel can shed as much as 5 pounds (2 kg) of hair at each molt.

• **HUMP** Contrary to popular belief, a camel does not store water in its hump. The hump is a mound of fatty tissue from which the animal draws energy when food is hard to find. When a camel uses its hump fat for sustenance, the mound becomes flabby and shrinks. If a camel draws too much fat, the small remaining lump will flop from its upright position and hang down the camel's side. Food and a few days' rest will return the hump to its normal firm condition.

• **LIFE SPAN** After a gestation period of 13 months, a camel cow usually bears a single calf, and occasionally twins. Calves walk within hours of birth but remain close to their mothers until they reach maturity at five years of age. The normal life span of a camel is 40 years, although a working camel retires from active duty at 25.

• **WATER** Although camels can withstand severe dehydration, a large one can drink as much as 28 gallons (106 l) in 10 minutes. Such an amount would kill another mammal, but the camel's unique metabolism enables the animal to store the water in its bloodstream.

buildings blend gracefully with classic Turkish and Islamic architecture in the midst of modern high-rises and businesses. Algiers is the site of the University of Algiers (established in 1879). Notable buildings include the Grand Mosque (built in the 11th century) and the national library.

The old Ottoman harbor is Algeria's busiest port and the mainstay of the economy. Fishing boats, yachts, and the Algerian navy share the waters with vessels carrying products such as oil, wine, fruit, and vegetable exports from the surrounding agricultural regions. Iron ore is also exported, and the harbor serves as a refueling depot for large vessels. Turn-of-the-century buildings line the semicircular bay and lead to the business district immediately behind it. Cement, chemicals, and paper products are manufactured in the city.

The most colorful part of the city is the famous Casbah (KAHZ-bah), which is Arabic for "fortress." After Algeria gained independence, the government wanted to move residents to new housing and proclaim the Casbah a historic district, but Algerians protested, and the government capitulated. The area is alive with children playing in front of dilapidated homes. Narrow streets lead to the souk, or market, with stalls of crafts, fruits, vegetables, and freshly slaughtered sheep hung in rows.

ORAN

About 225 miles (360 km) west of Algiers, along the coast between Algiers and the Moroccan border, lies Oran (Wahran in Arabic). Oran sits on a high cliff plateau that plunges into the Mediterranean. The city's long history is reflected through the architecture of its old Spanish fortress, mosque, French-built port facilities, and Nouvelle Ville (New City). Oran has two universities, the Université d'Oran (established in 1965) and the University of Science and Technology of Oran (established in 1975).

Oran is Algeria's second-largest city and the one with the greatest European influence. First built as a breakwater by Arabs from Spain in 903, the city later became a prosperous port under the Almohads and the subsequent Spanish occupation from the 16th to 18th centuries. The French designed Oran as Algeria's major second city, which had, until recently, more cathedrals than mosques.

Oran has a frontage road lined with palm trees along the Mediterranean. Elegant French-style houses mix with modern office and apartment buildings overlooking an imposing bay and busy harbor.

CONSTANTINE

Known to Phoenicians as Cirta, meaning "city," present-day Constantine is the capital of the Constantine province in northeastern Algeria. Algeria's third-largest city, Constantine is home to many of the most outstanding Roman ruins in the world. The straight streets, wide squares, and administrative buildings of the city's northwest sector speak of its Roman and French heritage. The Arab sector in the southeast is characterized by winding streets and craft markets.

Located 50 miles (80 km) inland near the Tunisian border, Constantine stretches over the top of a huge chalk cliff and is dramatically cut off from the surrounding plateau on three sides by the Rhumel River gorge.

Probably founded in prehistoric times, Constantine was the prosperous capital of Numidia under the powerful King Massinissa by the third century B.C. In A.D. 313 the city was renamed for the Roman emperor Constantine I, who rebuilt the city after it was destroyed in the war preceding his accession. Frequently contested by various Muslim dynasties, Constantine fell to the Turks in the 16th century and to the French in 1837.

HISTORY

THE INHABITANTS OF THE COASTAL AREA of present-day Algeria shared in an early Neolithic culture that was common to the whole Mediterranean littoral, or coast, before the 15th century B.C. South of the Atlas Mountains, nomadic hunters and herders roamed the vast savanna, abounding in game, that between 8000 and 2000 B.C. stretched across what is now the Sahara. Most of the savanna people scattered south and east into the Sudan region before the encroaching desert and invading horsemen. Others may have migrated northward, where they were eventually absorbed by the Berbers.

The origin of the Berbers is a mystery. Research has produced an abundance of educated speculation without any definitive solution. Many theories abound relating the Berbers to the Canaanites, the Phoenicians, the Celts, the Basques, and the Caucasians. Linguistic evidence suggests that the Berber languages form a branch of Afro-Asiatic languages that include Egyptian, Semitic, and Cushitic languages. Although it is still disputed which branches of Afro-Asiatic are the closest to Berber, most linguists agree on Semitic and Chadic.

CARTHAGE

Minoan seamen from Crete may have set up depots on the coast of present-day Algeria before 2000 B.C., but it was only with the arrival of Phoenician traders, who penetrated the western Mediterranean before the 12th century B.C., that the region entered into recorded history. Eventually Punic trading posts were established along the African coast, where the merchants of Tyre and, later, Carthage developed commercial relations with the Berber tribes of the interior and paid them tribute to ensure their cooperation in the exploitation of raw materials.

French paleontologist Camille Arambourg discovered the skeletal and cultural remains of Ternifine man (a type of prehistoric man) near Oran in 1954–55.

Opposite: **The Martyrs Monument in Algiers was erected in remembrance of those who died in the country's war for independence from French occupation. The war lasted from 1954 to 1962.**

TASSILI N'AJJER

Tassili n'Ajjer (tah-see-LEE nahd-JAIR), a plateau in the Saharan area of southern Algeria, is where French soldier Lieutenant Brenans discovered a large group of prehistoric rock paintings (*pictured here*) during a canyon operation in 1933. His discovery attracted the attention of French archaeologist Henri Lhote, who followed Brenans to examine the paintings. He then brought a team of painters and photographers to the plateau in 1956 to copy and record the discovery. The paintings in Tassili n'Ajjer's rock shelters and caves are about 8,000 years old, dating back to a time when hunter-gatherers and pastoralists flourished in a Sahara that enjoyed a much higher level of rainfall.

Painted over a period dating from 6000 B.C. to the first centuries of the present era, they are the most complete existing record of a prehistoric African culture and among the most remarkable Stone Age remains to be found anywhere. In a wide variety of styles ranging from naturalistic to abstract, the rock paintings depict the wild Saharan fauna and herds of domestic cattle and sheep. The inhabitants of the cave used a distinctive type of pottery known as Dotted Wavy Line, as well as ground and polished stone axes and adzes. Although they cultivated cereal crops, they also relied on hunting, gathering, and fishing in shallow lakes for much of their diet. The culture depicted in the rock paintings flourished until the region began to dry up as a result of climatic changes after 4000 B.C., but the prehistoric savanna has been described as the nursery for subsequent African civilization. The Tassili art is important for the light it throws on prehistoric migrations and economic practices in the Saharan savanna.

By the fifth century B.C. Carthage, the greatest of the overseas Punic colonies, had extended its hegemony across much of North Africa. Defeated in the long Punic Wars (third century B.C.), Carthage was reduced by Rome to the status of a small and vulnerable African state at the mercy of the Berber tribes, but its influence on North Africa remained strong.

BERBER KINGDOMS

The basic unit of social and political organization among the Berbers was the extended family, usually identified with a particular village or traditional grazing grounds. Families in turn were bound together in the clan. An alliance of clans, often tracing their origins to a common ancestor as a symbol of unity, formed a tribe. Because war was a permanent feature of tribal life, kindred tribes joined in confederations that were, in time, institutionalized for mutual defense. Some chieftains, successful in battle, established rudimentary territorial states, but their kingdoms were easily fragmented, and dynasties rarely survived a generation. By the second century B.C., however, several large but loosely administered Berber kingdoms had emerged. Two kingdoms were established in Numidia, the Massyli in the east and Massaesyli in the west, behind the coastal areas controlled by Carthage.

There are many Roman ruins still in Algeria, such as these at Guelma in northeast Algeria.

ISLAM AND THE ARABS

The most significant influence on Berber culture was the result of the Arab invasions in the seventh and 11th centuries. By the time of his death in 632, Prophet Muhammad and his followers had brought most of the tribes and towns of the Arabian Peninsula under the banner of Islam. Within a generation Arab armies had carried Islam westward across North Africa as far as Tripolitania. There stiff Berber resistance slowed the Arab advance, and efforts at permanent conquest were resumed only when it became apparent that the Maghrib could be opened up as a theater of operations in the Muslim campaign against the Byzantine Empire.

In 670 the Arabs surged into the Roman province of Africa, where they founded the city of Al Qayrawan 100 miles (160 km) south of Carthage. Pushed back onto their own resources, the Berber farmers of Numidia looked once again to the tribal chieftains for leadership. For a time the Arab advance was halted and Al Qayrawan put on the defensive, but by

Muslim Spain and the Maghrib, which had been conquered within 50 years of the founding of Al Qayrawan, were organized under the political and religious leadership of the Umayyad caliph of Damascus.

the end of the century fresh Arab troops, reinforced by newly converted Muslim Berber auxiliaries, had subdued the Numidian countryside. The last pockets of Byzantine resistance on the North African coast were wiped out only after the Arabs had obtained naval supremacy in the Mediterranean.

Sedentary Berber tribespeople turned now to the Arabs for protection against their nomadic kin. Berbers differed essentially from the Arabs in their political culture, however, and their communal and representative institutions contrasted sharply with the personal and authoritarian government of the Arabs. Even after their conversion to Islam, Berber tribes retained their customary laws in preference to Islamic law.

The Arabs formed an urban elite in the Maghrib, where they had come as conquerors and missionaries, not as colonists. Their armies traveled without women and married among the sedentary Berbers, propagating Arab culture and Islam among the townspeople and the farmers. Although conversion to Islam was more rapid among the nomadic tribes of the hinterland, paradoxically they were also the ones who stoutly resisted Arab political domination. The Berbers adapted Islam to their local culture, and this ultimately distinguished them from Muslim central powers who tried to assert government control.

The Kharijite movement surfaced in Morocco as a revolt against the Arabs in 739. The Berber Kharijites ("seceders," from the Arabic *khuruj*, meaning "abandonment") proclaimed that any suitable Muslim candidate could be elected caliph without regard to his race, station, or descent from the Prophet. The Kharijites challenged the Arab monopoly on religious leadership, and Berbers across the Maghrib rose in revolt in the name of religion against Arab domination. In the wake of the revolt, Kharijite

TIMGAD

The ruins of Timgad (ancient Thamugadi), in northeastern Algeria about 220 miles (350 km) southeast of Algiers, are the most complete of all the Roman centers in North Africa. The ruins are one of the best examples of the grid plan that was used in Roman city planning. Excavation begun by a French team in 1881 laid bare the entire plan of the colony. Founded in A.D. 100 by Emperor Trajan as a settlement for army veterans, Thamugadi was sited in rich farmland. The settlement prospered through commerce and agriculture; by A.D. 150 it had grown beyond its walls into the surrounding countryside. The Vandals sacked it in the fifth century.

The site's plan resembles a military camp, but it was designed for civilian occupation. The walls enclose a square area, 1,165 feet (355 m) per side, divided into quadrants by two colonnaded avenues and subdivided by a grid of streets. The crowding of temples, smaller baths, markets, offices, a theater, and houses within the walls forced many of the larger structures, especially the bigger baths, outside. Almost none of the sculptures exist today; the only remnants of the Roman architecture are the mosaic floors.

sectarians established a number of theocratic tribal kingdoms, most of which had short histories.

One of these kingdoms, the Rustumid dynasty (761–909), extended its rule over most of the central Maghrib. The Rustumids gained a reputation throughout the Islamic world for honesty and justice as well as for the openness and egalitarian nature of their imams (prayer leaders of a mosque). The court at Tahert (present-day Tiaret) was noted for its patronage of learning in mathematics, astronomy, and astrology as well as theology and law, but the Rustumid imams failed, by choice or by neglect, to organize a reliable standing army. This important factor, accompanied by the dynasty's eventual lapse into decadence, opened the way for Tahert's demise under the assault of the Fatimids.

FATIMIDS

In the closing decade of the ninth century, missionaries of the Ismaili sect of Shi'a Islam converted the Kutama Berbers of the Kabylia region and led them on a jihad against the Sunni rulers of Ifriqiya. Al Qayrawan fell to the Kutama Berbers in 909, and the next year the Kutama installed the Ismaili grand master from Syria as imam of their movement and ruler

over their territory. The imam initiated the Fatimid dynasty, named after Fatima, daughter of Muhammad, from whom he claimed descent.

The Fatimids turned westward in 911, destroying the Kharijite imamate at Tahert and claiming the central Maghrib for Shi'ism. Kharijite refugees fled south into the desert. They settled in the M'zab Valley.

For many years the Fatimids posed a threat to Morocco, but eventually they turned their attention eastward. By 969 they had completed the conquest of Egypt and moved their capital to the new city that they founded at Cairo, where they established a Shi'a caliphate.

ALMORAVIDS

The Almoravids ruled North Africa and Spain from 1056 to 1147. The dynasty originated in the western Sahara among the Berbers. From the mouth of the Senegal River, warriors spread a simple, fundamentalist form of Islam; they moved northward into Morocco and conquered North Africa as far as Algiers. Marrakesh was founded as the capital about 1062.

In 1086 the Almoravids crossed into Spain, defeated the Christian army, and annexed the territories of Muslim Spain. These rugged Berber nomads were conquered in turn by the refined civilization of Spain and were unable to defend their empire against the Almohads, another Berber dynasty, who killed the last Almoravid ruler in 1147.

ALMOHADS

The Almohads ruled North Africa and Spain from 1130 to 1269. The dynasty originated in a mass movement led by Ibn Tumart, a messianic leader who proclaimed himself the Mahdi (meaning in Arabic the "Rightly Guided One," expected to come before Judgment Day and the end of time) come to purify Islam. His successor, Abd al-Mumin, defeated the Almoravids and captured the Almoravid capital of Marrakesh in 1147. Subsequently all the Muslim territory in Spain was occupied, and North Africa was conquered as far as Tripolitania by 1160.

The Almohad court was a center of art and Arabic learning, yet the empire soon crumbled because of its great size, social divisions, and religious conservatism. Externally the Almohads were confronted by the Christian reconquest of Spain; their defeat at Las Navas de Tolosa in 1212 resulted in their total withdrawal from Spain. In North Africa, the empire divided into local kingdoms, called the Barbary States, one of which captured Marrakesh in 1269.

In the late 15th century Christian Spain, having expelled the Muslims from the Iberian Peninsula, captured several Algerian ports. The Christians were forced off the coast with Turkish assistance, and Algeria became nominally part of the Ottoman Empire in 1518, although the local rulers had a high degree of autonomy. The Barbary States were in fact conquered for Turkey by a corsair, or pirate, known as Barbarossa, to prevent their falling to Christian Spain. Thereafter, the Barbary States became a base

Fleeing Kharijites settled in oases in the M'zab region, founding cities where their descendants remain today.

Opposite: **A Berber woman and her child in traditional garb.**

25

for piracy against European shipping in the Mediterranean. The booty and the tribute paid to gain immunity from attacks was the chief revenue for local rulers.

Piracy against European shipping led to British and U.S. intervention in the early 19th century. In 1801 the United States, whose ships had been attacked, launched the Tripolitan War against Tripoli (now Libya). In 1815 the United States also fought against Algiers, which was bombarded by an Anglo-Dutch fleet in 1816. However, the piracy was effectively ended

HILALIANS

Despite their immense influence, the earliest Muslim Arabs in the Maghrib represented only a small urban elite, whose detribalized members frequently married Berber women or took wives from their own narrow circle of Arab families, which were the products of generations of intermarriage with Berbers. From the 12th to the 14th centuries, however, Arabs of a distinctly different character—tribal people known as the Hilalians—arrived in the Maghrib in large numbers, dramatically altering the face and culture of the region.

In the middle of the 11th century, the Fatimid caliph in Cairo invited the Bani Hilal and the Bani Salim, bedouin tribes originally from Hejaz, and the Yemen, who for years had ravaged upper Egypt, to migrate to the Maghrib and punish their rebellious vassals, the Zirids. The slow but continuous advance of these nomads across the region was like a "swarm of locusts," impoverishing it, destroying towns, and turning farmland into steppes, as described by the 14th-century Muslim historian Ibn Khaldun.

The Hilalian impact on the central Maghrib was devastating in both demographic and economic terms. Over a long period of time Arabs displaced Berber farmers from their land and converted it to pasturage. For the first time the extensive use of Arabic spread to the countryside. Sedentary Berbers who sought protection from the Hilalians were gradually Arabized. Others, driven from their traditional lands, joined them as nomads or fled to the mountains. Ironically, the first entry of these Arabs into Morocco in the 12th century coincided with a political and religious revival among the Berber tribal confederations.

only with the French conquest of Algeria in 1830 and the deposition of the dey (regent) of Algiers.

FRENCH RULE AND THE RISE OF NATIONALISM

The French brought in more than 100,000 troops in a campaign to conquer northern Algeria. This military onslaught devastated the Algerians and their crops and livestock. As the strongholds of Algerian leader Abd al-Qadir fell to the French, he was forced to surrender in 1847. By 1848 nearly all of northern Algeria was under French control. Despite fierce resistance, smaller French operations continued, pushing gradually southward until Algeria's current boundaries were drawn in 1907. France's protracted invasion of Algeria came at a high price: An estimated one-third of the entire Algerian population fell between the start of the invasion and the mid-1870s.

Algerian nationalist movements arose after World War I under the leadership of two men: Ahmed Ben Messali Hadj, who desired complete independence, and the moderate Ferhat Abbas, who wanted France to live up to its assimilationist ideas. European settlers, however, resisted all efforts to grant political and economic equality to the Algerians.

World War II aroused nationalist hopes, and when these were not met, strife broke out in Algeria. In 1945, when Algerians demonstrated for independence in Sétif and Constantine, the police opened fire, killing thousands. In retaliation Algerians organized armed groups and attacked European *colons* (koh-LOHN) or immigrants. French reprisal was swift. Altogether 103 French and 8,000 Algerians were killed. Although the French government granted Algerians the right to vote on a separate electoral roll in 1947, demands for full political equality and further reform were opposed.

Algeria suffered from bomb damage during World War II. During the early years of the war, Algeria was under the Vichy administration. After 1942, it served as a major base for the Allied North Africa campaign. Algiers was the capital of free France until the liberation of Paris.

THE WAR OF INDEPENDENCE

French rule had produced an Algeria in which European-style cities stood alongside centuries-old villages; large-scale agricultural units existed next to hundreds of tiny farms. More than a million European settlers *(colons)*—a majority of French origin—possessed the principal industrial, commercial, and agricultural enterprises. Most of the 8.5 million Muslims either pursued primitive economic activities or performed menial tasks in the modern sector. Despite reforms and the fact that Algeria was technically not a colony but comprised three departments of France, the Muslims were politically disadvantaged as well. They had equality before the law but little power to make or administer the law.

Nationalist aspirations for liberation heightened Muslim discontent. The Front de Libération Nationale (FLN), or National Liberation Front, was formed, and on November 1, 1954, small FLN bands began to raid French army installations and *colons'* holdings.

The FLN also used revolutionary war and terror tactics to force adherence by the Muslims or to dissuade them from apathy or sympathy toward the French. Terror begat terror; the French army responded with traditional and counterrevolutionary military methods. But the French had little success. Neither the military efforts of the 500,000-strong army nor sizable political concessions produced a decisive defeat of the rebels or the firm allegiance of the Muslim masses. By 1958 the Fourth Republic was at a stalemate—and in crisis.

The *colons* and certain factions of the French army were alarmed by the ineffectiveness of the Paris government. On May 13, 1958, in Algiers, the Algerians rioted, overran the government offices, and established an emergency Committee of Public Safety. In Paris, Premier Pierre Pflimlin's ministry was paralyzed, and Charles de Gaulle was asked to become premier. He was granted emergency powers and the right to frame a constitution for a Fifth Republic.

In 1962, in the face of international disapproval and turmoil in France, de Gaulle finally announced a referendum on independence. After an overwhelming vote in favor of independence and in spite of violent protests by French nationals, Algeria became independent on July 5, 1962. Algeria was the last of the French holdings in North Africa to become independent, Tunisia and Morocco having achieved that status in 1956. After a power struggle within the FLN, Mohamed Ahmed Ben Bella became Algeria's first president, in 1963.

INDEPENDENCE AND AFTER

Confronting a society devastated by war and the subsequent flight of European capital and skilled workers, Ben Bella nationalized abandoned colonial holdings and announced his support of national liberation movements in other colonial lands. Conflict with Morocco, economic difficulties, and Ben Bella's dictatorial personality provoked a bloodless coup led by Houari Boumédienne on June 19, 1965. Boumédienne maintained Algeria's image as an avant-garde Third World state and began its support of demands for an independent Western Sahara. His nationalization of French oil and natural gas concessions in 1971 symbolized Algeria's economic liberation, but Algeria still accepted French aid.

Chadli Bendjedid, who became president in 1979 after the death of Boumédienne in 1978 and was elected in 1984 and 1988, maintained Algeria's prominence as a speaker for the Third World and pursued Maghrib unity. He liberalized the economy somewhat, but high unemployment, inflation, and corruption sparked massive unrest in October 1988.

The ban on new political parties was lifted in 1989, and opposition parties were allowed to take part in future elections. At the time, the Front Islamique du Salut (FIS), or Islamic Salvation Front, was founded. This party advocated the establishment of Islamic law and government. More than 20 licenses were issued to other newly formed political parties as well. In the June 1990 local elections—the first multiparty elections since 1962—FIS won 54 percent of the vote. In 1991 the Algerian government announced that national elections would be held in June 1991 and restricted political campaigning in mosques. The FIS responded by staging violent protests and calling for a general strike to demand an Islamic state. This led the Algerian government to impose a state of siege from June to September, and FIS leaders were arrested and imprisoned.

In December 1991 the FIS won the first round of delayed legislative elections and was certain to obtain a majority in the second round. In January 1992 the National People's Assembly was dissolved by presidential decree, and subsequently Chadli Bendjedid was forced to step down due to pressure from army leaders. The army seized control, canceled the runoff elections, and installed Mohamed Boudiaf as head of a new presidential council. Public gatherings were forbidden, and the FIS fought against the military, which resulted in the declaration of a state of emergency. The FIS was ordered to disband and outlawed with the dissolution of all 411 FIS-controlled local and regional authorities.

Boudiaf was assassinated in June 1992 by one of his bodyguards, who was alleged to have Islamic links, and a full-scale civil war broke out. Violence escalated, and Islamic extremists warned foreigners to leave Algeria or risk death. Many civilians were massacred, and the Armed Islamic Group (GIA) appeared to be responsible for these operations. During this Algerian civil war, the military rulers appointed Liamine Zéroual, a retired colonel, as chairman of the Higher State Council in 1994. He also won a five-year presidential term in 1995 with a clear majority of votes. Thus, he became Algeria's fourth head of state in two years.

In 1998 President Zéroual shortened his term and held early presidential elections. The following year Abdelaziz Bouteflika, the former foreign minister, won 74 percent of the votes. In September 2000 his proposed Law on Civil Harmony, granting amnesty to all insurgents not guilty of rape and murder, was approved in a nationwide referendum. Violence in Algeria declined to manageable levels. Bouteflika was reelected for another five years in 2004 in recognition of his efforts in stabilizing the country. He soon passed another referendum in 2005, the Charter for Peace and National Reconciliation, together with a second amnesty offer. Although Bouteflika's economic reforms are not progressing as fast as the people had hoped, Algerians acknowledged his ability to pacify Islamic militants, and recently Algeria has experienced a decrease in violence.

Mohamed Ahmed Ben Bella was an idealist loved by the people of Algeria.

31

GOVERNMENT

THE NATIONAL LIBERATION FRONT (FLN) led Algeria to independence and was the country's only legal political party until 1989. The 1963 constitution was suspended following a military coup in 1965. A 1976 constitution provided for a unicameral National Assembly and a powerful president. A new national charter, approved in 1986, increased the role of the private sector and declared socialism and Islam to be the twin pillars of the state. In November 1988 after a wave of antigovernment protests, voters overwhelmingly approved increasing the power of the prime minister, who was made responsible to the legislature, and reducing the role of the FLN. In February 1989 they approved a new constitution that paved the way for the July 1989 legalization of a multiparty system.

The constitution was amended again in 1996 to outlaw political parties founded along religious, linguistic, racial, regional, or sexist lines. This ensured that public rights and freedom were protected. It may also have been added to eliminate the possible emergence of Islamic, Berber, or regional parties that might have mounted credible opposition. The High Court, established in 1996, was empowered to judge the president on high treason and the prime minister for crimes and offenses.

Algeria today is a constitutional republic with a democratically elected government. The government exercises executive power, and legislative power is bicameral; the two chambers of parliament are the National People's Assembly and the Council of Nation. Algeria's judicial system is based on French and Islamic law. Algeria recently ended an 11-year

Above: **French forces guarding a control point during the Algerian War of Independence between 1954 and 1962.**

Opposite: **An Algerian boy casts his father's vote during the presidential elections of 2004.**

33

civil war caused by political, economic, and social turmoil. The end of the war was often credited to Abdelaziz Bouteflika, who took over as president and proposed national reconciliation by granting amnesty to all armed militants.

CIVIL WAR

Political, social, and economic problems created a climate of violent unrest in Algeria. The conflict began in December 1991, when the first-round electoral results showed the fundamentalist Islamic Salvation Front (FIS) winning by a large margin. Fearing that the FIS would dismantle the democratic system that had enabled its ascendance, the army seized control, canceled the runoff elections, and outlawed the FIS. Other Islamic rebel groups soon emerged, and civil war broke out. Assassinations of Algerian intellectuals, government officials, journalists, and military officers were frequent, as were campaigns against foreigners. Sporadic bombings, gun battles between government forces and insurgents, and other violence occurred almost daily. Algerian military and other security personnel were unable to offer adequate protection.

The government of Algeria imposed a rigorously enforced late-night curfew in the central region around Algiers. Roadblocks were located at many major intersections. In response, terrorist groups set up false roadblocks as ambushes.

More than 100 foreigners were kidnapped and murdered after September 1993, sometimes in assaults involving dozens of attackers. A terrorist attack at a pipeline facility south of Algiers resulted in the death of five expatriates. Terrorists threatened to kill all foreigners who did not leave Algeria. An Air France flight was hijacked at the

Algiers airport on December 24, 1994, by heavily armed terrorists who threatened to blow up the aircraft. Women as well as intellectuals, writers, journalists, and artists were a particular target of the terrorists.

By mid-1994 three special courts instituted to try suspects accused of terrorist offenses had handed down some 490 death sentences, and 26 executions had been carried out in an effort to curb the violence. Amnesty International has condemned the Algerian government for widespread use of torture and systematic killing of suspected militants.

Despite threats to their lives, 75 percent of Algerian citizens in Algeria and overseas disregarded the Islamists' calls to boycott the November 1995 elections and elected Liamine Zéroual president.

Violence peaked in 1997, when the government armed vigilante groups to attack those suspected to be from Islamic rebel groups. In response, guerrillas massacred hundreds in the villages of Bentalha, Bou Rhais, and Beni Messous. The civil war cost tens of billions of dollars in damages to factories, other buildings, and transportation routes and left close to 100,000 people, mostly civilians, dead. A government crisis ensued, and President Zéroual stepped down in 1999.

Abdelaziz Bouteflika took over and focused on restoring stability and security to the country. His Law on Civil Harmony granted amnesty to all insurgents not guilty of rape and murder. It was estimated that 85 percent of those fighting the regime accepted the amnesty. In 2002 the surrender of the Islamic Salvation Army and the defeat of the Armed

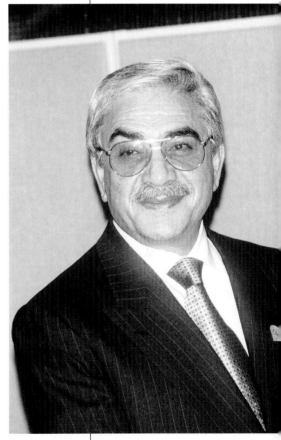

Former Algerian president, Liamine Zéroual.

The former building of the FLN party in Tizi-Ouzou in Kabylia.

Islamic Group brought an end to the 11-year civil conflict. Bouteflika also addressed Berber demands for greater cultural and political recognition. In 2001 the government recognized Tamazight, the Berber language, as one of Algeria's national languages and has offered to sponsor the teaching of the Berber language in schools. This is a politically significant move that signaled a greater official recognition for the Berber minority after years of French colonization and Arab nationalism. Although security in the nation has improved, low-level fighting still continues in some areas, mainly in the mountainous part of the east.

GOVERNMENT STRUCTURE

The president is the head of state and the head of the armed forces and is responsible for national defense. He must be Algerian, a Muslim, and at least 40 years old. If he is married, his wife must also be Algerian. Although it is not explicitly conveyed in Algerian law, it is nationally assumed that the presidential candidate has to be male. Yet in 2004 an Algerian woman unsuccessfully ran for president.

The president is elected by secret ballot for a five-year term and can be reelected only once. The president presides over a Council of Ministers and the High Security Council. He decides and conducts foreign policy. He appoints a prime minister, who initiates legislation and appoints his own Council of Ministers. The Algerian legislation is bicameral, consisting of the National People's Assembly (APN, from its French name) and the Council of Nation. All of the APN's 389 members are elected by popular vote to serve a five-year term. Regional and municipal authorities elect two-thirds of the upper chamber, the Council of Nation, while the president elects the other one-third. Members are required to serve a six-year term, and the constitution requires that half of the council be renewed every three years. When the APN is not in session, the president can legislate by decree, after consulting with the prime minister.

The National People's Assembly proposes and, with the Council of Nation, ratifies laws. The APN has two ordinary sessions per year, though it may be convened for an extraordinary session at the request of the president, the prime minister, or two-thirds of its members. Both the prime minister and the APN may initiate legislation.

THE CONSTITUTION

The constitution can be revised on the initiative of the president by a two-thirds majority of the National People's Assembly and the approval of voters in a national referendum. The basic principles of the constitution may not be revised. The constitution was last revised in November 1996. Among its revisions was the creation of a bicameral legislation. It also reconfirmed the prohibition of institutions based on regionalist and feudalistic practices or practices that are contrary to Islamic ethics.

The state guarantees the inviolability of the home, of private life, and of the person. The state also guarantees secrecy of correspondence; freedom of conscience and opinion; freedom of intellectual, artistic, and scientific creation; and freedom of expression and assembly.

The state guarantees the right to form political associations, to join a trade union, to strike, to work, to protection, to security, to health, to leisure, and to education. It also guarantees the right to leave the national territory, within the limits set by law.

PRESIDENT ABDELAZIZ BOUTEFLIKA

Amid protests of vote rigging, Bouteflika first took office in 1999 with the backing of the army. He is known for restoring peace to the country and also for the success of his civil concord offering amnesty to insurgents. He was voted to serve Algeria for another term in 2004. In his charter for peace and reconciliation in 2005, he passed a second amnesty for the remaining militants.

Bouteflika is a veteran of the war for independence from France. He served as Algeria's foreign minister for 16 years, until 1979. He was expected to succeed President Houari Boumédienne in 1979 but was passed over in favor of Chadli Bendjedid. He was later accused of corruption during his diplomatic career, and he went into self-imposed exile for several years. Those charges were later dropped.

The constitution perpetuates the 1984 Family Code, which relegated Algerian women to the status of minors for life, restricted their rights, and maintained the legal authority of men over women. Although President Bouteflika has announced revisions to the law, it has yet to be changed. In 2005 it was decreed that Algerian citizens have the right to dual citizenship. The constitution has named Islam as the state religion and Arabic as the only official national language. At the same time, the Berber language is recognized nationally as well as spoken by many Algerians, and French is a widely studied foreign language, with many university courses taught in French.

POLITICAL PARTIES AND ELECTIONS

From independence until 1989, the National Liberation Front (FLN) was the only authorized political grouping, Algeria having been designated as a one-party state. Under constitutional changes approved in 1989, however, Algerians were permitted to form "associations of a political nature" as long as they did not "threaten the basic interests of the state" and were not "created exclusively on the basis of religion, language, region, sex, race, or profession." In 1997 a law banning political parties based on religion was enforced; this was intended to avoid the reconstitution of religious extremists such as the FIS. To operate legally, parties were also required to obtain government permits. The process of legalization began in August 1989, and multiparty activity was permitted for the first time at a local election in June 1990. Today Algeria has more than 40 legal parties, all approved by the Ministry of the Interior.

A new electoral law, adopted in 1997, introduced a system of proportional representation for local elections. This meant that any list of candidates obtaining more than 30 percent of the votes would win two-thirds of the seats in parliament.

Following a proposal by the political party el-Islah, or the Movement for National Reform, electoral procedures were amended in 2004. The amendment abolished the special voting college for army officers, obliging them to vote alongside other citizens.

SOME LEGAL PARTIES

Leader of the Islamic Salvation Front, Cheikh Abassi Madani, at a press conference in April 1990.

NATIONAL LIBERATION FRONT (Front de Libération Nationale, FLN). For many years this was the only political party in Algeria. Even with the introduction of a multiparty system, this party still dominates Algerian politics, with 199 members in parliament.

MOVEMENT FOR NATIONAL REFORM (Mouvement du Rénouveau National, MRN; Arabic, el-Islah). A moderate Islamic party with 43 members in parliament. Party leader Saad Abdallah Djaballah ran for president in 1999 and 2004.

NATIONAL RALLY FOR DEMOCRACY (Rassemblement National Démocratique, RND). Created in 2005, RND is a member of a three-party political alliance called the Presidential Alliance. Its other two members are the Movement for the Society of Peace (formerly Hamas) and the FLN. This party is loyal to President Bouteflika.

MOVEMENT FOR THE SOCIETY OF PEACE (Mouvement de la Société pour la Paix, MSP). The party was formerly called Hamas, and it has

38 members in parliament. The party advocates "coexistence" with groups of opposing views and introducing "by stages" an Islamic state that would maintain "respect for individual liberties."

MILITANT GROUPS

The Salafist Group for Preaching and Combat (Groupe Salafiste pour la Prédication et le Combat, GSPC) is a militant Islamic group that aims to overthrow the Algerian government and institute an Islamic state. Hassan Hattab founded the group in 1998 after he broke away from the Armed Islamic Group (GIA), another militant underground fundamentalist organization.

Many insurgents surrendered when Bouteflika offered amnesty in 1999, which neutralized much of the GIA's and GSPC's support. However, some members of the GSPC are still active in the forests of western Kabylia, in eastern Algeria, assassinating police and army personnel in the area. The GSPC also expanded into the Sahara. In 2003 a splinter group of the GSPC, the Free Salafist Group (GSL), kidnapped 32 European tourists as they were traveling through the Sahara.

Some reports have alleged that Hattab had lost his leadership role in GSPC after 2001 and was replaced by Nabil Sahraoui. There were also reports that Hattab called on members of the GSPC to disarm and take up the second amnesty offered by Bouteflika. According to reports, about 400 GSPC members surrendered.

The GSPC has yet to disband completely and has been identified as a Foreign Terrorist Organization by the U.S. Department of State. In 2006 the GSPC formed a union with Al-Qaeda, another Islamic organization, to work together against French and American interests. Emir Abu Musab Abdelwadoud now heads the GSPC.

ECONOMY

ABOUT 3.17 PERCENT OF ALGERIA'S LAND, mostly along the coast, is arable. The country has petroleum deposits and the eighth-largest natural gas reserves in the world. There are also deposits of iron ore, phosphates, mercury, uranium, and zinc.

During the colonial period, Algeria's major exports were wines and citrus fruits. That changed when the discovery of Saharan petroleum and natural gas in the mid-1950s accelerated French investment and initiated the ongoing transformation of the Algerian economy. The oil boom in the 1960s and 1970s greatly benefited Algeria, and the Five-Year Plan (1984–89) that followed soon after encouraged private and foreign investment in the country. In 1971 almost all foreign enterprises were nationalized, including French oil and natural gas interests. The economy, particularly the production and distribution of petroleum, natural gas, and

An estimated 10.15 million of Algeria's workforce was unemployed in 2005.

Left: **Small businesses such as this shop are common in Algeria.**

Opposite: **The busy port of Algiers bustles with incoming and outgoing cargo.**

43

minerals, remains largely under state control, despite the return of some land and businesses to private hands in the 1980s.

Although Algeria today continues to diversify its economy, it is still dependent on oil and gas exports to finance internal development. The recent oil price hikes in 2000 and 2001 not only helped Algeria increase its trade surplus but also reduced its foreign debt. Despite its wealth in oil, Algeria still suffers from a high unemployment rate of 17.1 percent and a severe housing shortage. A quarter of its population is estimated to live below the poverty line.

MINING AND OTHER INDUSTRIES

Industry (including mining, manufacturing, construction, and power) contributed an estimated 60 percent of the gross domestic product (GDP) in 2005 and engaged 13.4 percent of the employed population in manufacturing, 10 percent in construction and public works, and 14.6 percent in trade. Algeria's major mineral exports are petroleum and natural gas. Out of 1.9 million barrels of oil and natural gas produced per day in 2004, nearly 1.7 million barrels were exported. Algeria's largest oil field is the Hassi Messaoud in the Sahara Desert. It contributes about 400,000 barrels of oil per day. Reserves of iron ore, phosphates, lead, uranium, and zinc are also exploited. Algeria has deposits of antimony, tungsten, manganese, mercury, copper, and salt too.

Industry in Algeria has experienced a downward slide in recent years due to structural transformation from a government-controlled economy to a free-market one. Industrial production has fallen as inefficient plants are closed and oversize industries scaled down. The state owns about three-quarters of the manufacturing industry, which is operating at only 40 percent of its full capacity. In 2004 the manufacturing sector's contribution to the GDP was a mere 9 percent. Today Algeria's emphasis in the manufacturing industry has shifted from food processing and textiles to heavy industries such as steel and petrochemical works. There is a large steelworks in Annaba and gas liquefaction plants in Bejaïa and Arzew. The phosphate fertilizer factory in Annaba is a major component of Algeria's heavy-industrial development. Algeria has also made agreements with foreign companies to set up automobile assembly and engine production industries. Automobiles, trucks, cement, and rubber tires are major manufactures.

Much of the industrialized world's source of energy is derived from natural gas and petroleum. Given that energy prices have risen steadily in recent years, these natural resources now provide 95 percent of Algeria's export earnings. Algeria is a member of the Organization of Petroleum Exporting Countries (OPEC). Initial development plans, particularly the building of ultramodern petrochemical and gas liquefaction complexes to complement Algeria's oil and natural gas fields, have been successful. Currently Algeria has five refineries and an expanding petrochemicals industry concentrated in Skikda, Arzew, and Annaba. There are also four pipelines that transport petroleum from Algeria's oil fields to the Mediterranean for export overseas. In 2003 Algeria produced 27 billion kilowatt hours of electricity.

Algerian workers laying the Gazoduc Maghreb Pipeline.

Heavy harvests are tightly bundled and carried back by rural women living in the agricultural lands of Algeria.

AGRICULTURE

Agriculture (including forestry and fishing) contributed an estimated 10.1 percent to Algeria's GDP in 2005. Although the agricultural sector provided about 14 percent of Algeria's working population with employment, it has largely been neglected in terms of development. The sector suffers from underinvestment and poor organization. As a result, cereal production is subject to fluctuations, orchard and industrial crops have largely stagnated, and the fishing industry is underdeveloped. The recently ended civil strife that started in the early 1990s also hampered agricultural production. Food production has fallen well below the level of self-sufficiency. Algeria's modest agricultural activity combined with a growing population makes the country one of the world's largest agricultural import markets. Its imported food and agricultural products amount to about $2.8 billion a year.

The country's aridity has unfortunately rendered four-fifths of the land uncultivable. Cultivated land in Algeria is largely restricted to the coastal plains and valleys. The principal crops are wheat, barley, and oats. Olives, citrus fruits, grapes, vegetables, figs, and dates are also grown.

Air Algerie, the national airline, operates internationally.

Wine production has declined, as the government has uprooted many vineyards because of Islamic prohibitions and replaced them with plantings of cereal crops. The raising of livestock (mainly sheep and goats) provides a livelihood for nomads in sparsely settled semiarid areas.

TRANSPORTATION AND TRADE

The French left an impressive infrastructure, which the Algerians have maintained and expanded. The excellent road system now includes a trans-Saharan highway connecting northern Algeria with the far south and a rail network connecting Algeria to Morocco and Tunisia. Currently under construction are three big projects to build a tramway network in the cities of Algiers, Oran, and Constantine. Major ports include Oran, Arzew, Bejaïa, Skikda, Jijel, Algiers, Djendjene, Mostaganem, and Annaba.

Although France remains its primary trading partner, Algeria has successfully diversified its markets. Other major trading partners are Italy, Spain, Germany, the United States, China, Canada, Brazil, and Belgium. Currently there are two gas exportation pipelines. A trans-Mediterranean pipeline, completed in 1983, transports natural gas to Italy via Tunisia and Sicily. Another, the Maghreb-Europe Gas pipeline, completed in 1996, connects Algeria to Spain and Portugal via Morocco. Another two pipelines are in the works from Oran to Spain and eventually France; and another to Sardinia, Italy, from Annaba. Petroleum and natural gas are exported to the United States and other nations as well. Algeria's principal exports are mineral fuels, lubricants (including petroleum and derivatives), vegetables, tobacco, cork, hides, and dates. Principal imports include machinery and transport equipment, food, and consumer goods.

IMPROVING ECONOMIC OUTLOOK

Faced with declining oil revenues and high debts and interest payments in the early 1990s, Algeria's government embarked on an aggressive economic development plan to liberalize the economy, allow a greater measure of private enterprise, and encourage foreign investment. It also actively marketed hydrocarbons, especially natural gas, while promoting new hydrocarbon industries and agriculture.

Algeria's macroeconomic program was largely successful in narrowing its budget deficits and reducing inflation from nearly 30 percent in the 1990s to an estimated 1.9 percent in 2005. Its economy has grown an average of about 2.4 percent annually since 1999. In 2004 its economic growth was at 5.2 percent. Algeria has also managed to whittle down its foreign debts from $28 billion in 1999 to $21.8 billion in 2004. In 2006 Algeria decided to pay off in full its $8 billion debt to the Paris Club, a group of rich creditor nations, ahead of schedule.

The success of Algeria's economic plans was aided by rising oil prices in 1999, 2000, and 2004. In 2001 the government signed an association treaty with the European Union (EU) to lower tariffs and increase trade.

The agreement came into effect in September of the same year. Algeria continues to enjoy economic success, and the government pledges to persevere in its efforts to pursue key structural reforms such as continuing partial or complete privatization of state-owned enterprises and reducing government bureaucracy. Algeria is also working toward membership in the World Trade Organization. If successful, the country can look forward to improved international trade.

ORGANIZATION OF PETROLEUM EXPORTING COUNTRIES

The Organization of Petroleum Exporting Countries (OPEC) was created by Iran, Iraq, Kuwait, Saudi Arabia, and Venezuela in Baghdad on September 14, 1960, to counter the oil price cuts of U.S. and European oil companies. Qatar joined in 1961, Indonesia and Libya in 1962, Abu Dhabi (now part of the United Arab Emirates) in 1967, Algeria in 1969, Nigeria in 1971, and Ecuador and Gabon in 1973. In 1979 OPEC countries produced 66 percent of the world's petroleum, but by 2006 it was estimated that the OPEC members accounted for only 40 percent of world oil production and about two-thirds of the world's proven oil reserves.

In its first decade OPEC limited itself to preventing reductions in the price of oil, but by 1970 it had begun to press for rate increases (there was a fourfold increase in 1973–74 alone). Prices stabilized between 1974 and 1978 but increased by more than 100 percent during 1979. Demand slackened at the higher prices, and non-OPEC producers increased production. OPEC production quotas broke down during the 1980s, and there were disputes between nations seeking to curb production in hopes of driving prices up and those increasing production to avoid disrupting the world economy or to sustain earnings in the face of dropping prices. OPEC's influence continued to decline in the 1990s. Ecuador withdrew from the organization on January 1, 1993, and Gabon followed in 1995. With the newest addition of Angola in 2007, OPEC currently has 12 member nations. Although Iraq remains a member of OPEC, its oil production has not been a part of any OPEC quota agreements since March 1998. OPEC's current influence over crude oil prices continues to decline. Granted that, Algeria's heavy reliance on petroleum has made it extremely vulnerable to oil price fluctuations on the world market.

ENVIRONMENT

ALGERIA'S DRAMATICALLY VARIED COASTAL, mountainous, and grassy desert landscapes are home to a rich variety of wildlife—from antelopes and boars in the north to foxes and bats in the south. It is therefore unfortunate that global climate change during the past 30 years and centuries of careless environmental practices have resulted in not only a declining wildlife population but also the dangerous encroachment of the desert onto the country's fertile northern region. Other significant environmental issues threatening the fragile balance of Algeria's wildlife and the health of the human population include the improper dumping of industrial effluents and untreated sewage into the country's sea and rivers.

The development and conservation of the environment is therefore a central and vital issue for the Algerian government. Billions have been spent in developing national parks and reserves as well as in funding for organizations specializing in conservation in an effort to safeguard Algeria's natural resources. Although some early conservation policies did not meet with resounding success, Algeria remains confident that continued campaigns will educate the public, change people's environmental behavior, and instill in them the culture of conservation and preservation.

THE ENCROACHING DESERT

Advancing desert areas is not a problem specific to Algeria—it is also a serious global issue. Uncontrolled desertification could result in forced migration and create more than 135 million refugees worldwide. Various factors including the loss of biodiversity, poor human management of land, and climatic changes lead to desertification, a process in which productive land is turned into barren, desertlike areas.

Opposite: **The endangered gazelle in the Sahara Desert. Increasing desertification and the onslaught of persistent drought are threatening the biodiversity that Algeria is home to.**

This disturbing environmental issue in Algeria is evident in the northward encroachment of the Sahara Desert onto the fertile coastal and highland Tell and inland Saharan Atlas regions. Because most of Algeria is desert or semidesert, more than 90 percent of the population is forced to live on about 20 percent of the land. Each year Algeria loses 98,842 acres (40,000 ha) of its most fertile lands to desertification. During the past 10 years, more than 32 million acres (13 million ha) of territory has been affected by desertification. It is expected that in the coming year, the Sahara will have advanced within 124 miles (200 km) of Algeria's Mediterranean coastline.

Virtually all the land that can support life in Algeria is used for agriculture. As a result all but about 1.3 percent of the country's trees, a mix of pine and hardwood varieties, have been cut down and the land planted with crops. Indiscriminate and unauthorized deforestation, in addition to detrimental farming practices such as burning scrub vegetation, poor cropping techniques, and overgrazing, leave the soil exposed, inevitably leading to soil erosion. Soil erosion then accelerates Algeria's already serious problem of desertification.

Early efforts to combat desertification spanned a period of 20 years at the cost of $100 million per year. The "green wall" project, started back in 1975, covered an area 932 miles (1,500 km) long and 12 miles (20 km) wide along the northern fringes of the Sahara. Unfortunately this initiative failed due to continued deforestation and overgrazing on plant cover. Should these poor practices continue, they will only worsen the twin problems of food insufficiency and the exodus of the southern population to northern cities.

To address the above problems, the government is involved in an ongoing project to convert the southernmost 20 percent of Algeria's land into vineyards and fruit and olive orchards. Helmed by the Ministry of Agriculture, this project was started in December 2000 in the hope that the barrier of vegetation would halt the northwest movement of the Sahara and spare the fertile northern region from desertification.

Another body involved in slowing down desertification is the High Commission for Development of the Steppe (HCDS). Established in 1981, the HCDS is in charge of regenerating and protecting more than 79 million acres (32 million ha) of the Algerian steppe, which is approximately 124 miles (200 km) south of Algiers. Since the creation of the HCDS, about 6.4 million acres (2.6 million ha) of steppe have been restored. HCDS is in the process of restoring another 17.3 million acres (7 million ha) of steppe. The regeneration of the steppe has allowed more than 7 million of the steppe's residents to continue with their livelihood—taking care of their 18 million sheep—which is one of Algeria's sources of food security.

Environmentalists are also looking to create national parks in certain desert regions. Taghit, an oasis 700 miles (1,127 km) southwest of Algiers and 55 miles (89 km) southwest of Bechar, has been cited as an example. It has already drawn a large number of tourists because of its unspoiled natural environment. It is hoped that giving Taghit a protected status as a national park will not only contain desertification but also improve the standard of living of its local population.

Although various antidesertification projects have had some measure of success, desertification remains an urgent reality for the country. The Algerian government has pumped in another $2.5 billion for various agencies to continue with the development of the south. Algeria has also carried out research on desertification trends using satellite imagery in addition to holding national awareness workshops and developing government and nongovernmental organization (NGO) partnerships.

Algeria also seeks international solidarity in combating desertification. It has already signed and ratified the Rio Conventions on climate change and desertification. Other environmental treaty agreements supported by Algeria include the Kyoto Protocol on climate change and the Vienna Convention on ozone layer protection.

WATER POLLUTION

Another serious environmental issue plaguing Algeria is the contamination of its water due to the dumping of untreated sewage, industrial effluents, and pollutants from the oil industry. Although an estimated 90 percent of the urban population is connected to a sewage network, most of these wastewater treatment plants are out of service. Untreated sewage is thus discharged into natural bodies of water.

The dumping of waste from petrochemical industries is also rampant. To the country's east, particularly around Annaba and Skikda, Algeria's Mediterranean coast and rivers are heavily polluted with waste byproducts from paper mills, oils and soaps, heavy metals, and fertilizer runoff. It is estimated that nearly 261.6 million cubic yards (200 million cubic m) of untreated industrial wastewater is discharged into the environment each year. The coast of Bejaïa, for one, is heavily polluted with waste from a nearby vegetable oil factory. The World Bank has estimated that the annual cost of environmental damage on the coast of the Mediterranean is about 5 percent of Algeria's GDP.

Such environmental hazards constitute a constant threat not only to human life and livelihood but also to wildlife biodiversity. Several of Algeria's wetland sites in Ouargla, Batna, and Sétif are under threat because of water pollution. In a move to crack down on the continued uncontrolled industrial dumping and hydrocarbon pollution, a National Plan for the

ALGERIA'S ENDANGERED ANIMALS

Critically endangered animals today include the addax (an antelope) and the Mediterranean monk seal. The monk seal lives in caves and among rocky outcrops along the coast of Algeria. Attempts to increase the seal population have been slow and difficult because the seals are sensitive to disturbances. Pregnant females, who can give birth only to a single pup at a time, have been known to abort when disturbed. Overfishing and pollution of the Algerian waters have also drastically reduced the number of these seals. Other endangered or vulnerable animals include the wild dog, the serval (a midsize wild African cat), the Mediterranean horseshoe bat, and the Eurasian otter.

Management of Hazardous Waste (PNAGDES), spanning a period of 10 years, has been implemented. Established in 2001, PNAGDES calls for the elimination of dangerous waste such as asbestos, mercury, zinc sludge, plastic derivatives, pesticides, and excess oil from factories. It is hoped that such a move could reduce Algeria's yearly national production of 325,000 tons of hazardous waste from its petrochemical industry. PNAGDES also heavily taxes polluters in a bid to control indiscriminate dumping. In addition, the government has announced the closure of some 100 factories and arrested 120 people for violation of environmental standards in 2004. Other environmental bodies in charge of water planning, management, and monitoring as well as pollution control are the Ministry of Water Resources and the Ministry of Environment and Land Use Planning.

Algeria adheres to environmental conventions dealing with the pollution of the marine environment such as the UN Convention on the Laws of the Sea, the International Convention for the Prevention of Pollution from Ships (MARPOL), and the Basel Convention covering the transportation and disposal of hazardous waste. Algeria signed an agreement with Tunisia and Morocco on June 2005 to control marine pollution caused by accidents in the southwest Mediterranean Sea. Algeria is also committed to Horizon 2020, an initiative that aims to tackle the top sources of Mediterranean pollution by the year 2020.

A few servals are still found in the northern parts of Algeria, as their main habitat is the savanna. Rising human population and hunting for their pelts have led to these beautiful cats dwindling in number.

55

080959

Algeria's conservation efforts have been quite late, and some species have been severely affected. The dama gazelle is on the endangered list, and the scimitar-horned oryx is extinct in the wild, though some can still be found in captivity.

BIODIVERSITY

Algeria's diverse landscape, with its varied ecological zones, supports an amazing variety of wildlife. Ninety-two mammalian species can be found in the country. Wild boars, jackals, foxes, and gazelles are common animals, and although rare, small panthers, leopards, and cheetahs can be seen as well. The country is host to 183 species of breeding birds including the black-winged stilt, and the pied avocet, or *kluut*. Reptiles including snakes, and monitor lizards are plentiful throughout Algeria's semiarid regions.

However, the country's sparse vegetation can support only a limited wildlife population. The government realizes that it is crucial that endangered animals are protected under Algerian law. On October 19, 2006, a bill for the protection of endangered species was drafted. Included in the bill was a list of 23 wildlife species threatened with extinction. Sanctions against hunting, trapping, transporting, and trading in these endangered species have been implemented. It is only under exceptional circumstances, such as scientific purposes or to facilitate breeding, that the mentioned species are allowed to be used.

As of 2003, 29 million acres (11.7 million ha) of the country, including numerous national parks, nature reserves, wetlands, and biosphere reserves, had been protected. Although many Algerian wildlife programs are still in the midst of being properly established, a number have already been instituted. However, they do not all deal solely with Algerian wildlife. Three of these programs are the Preservation Station, the Peregrine Fund, and the International Fund for Animal Welfare (IFAW). The Preservation Station is dedicated to the captive breeding of tamed felines. Their young are then introduced into the wild. The Preservation Station's flagship species is the Barbary lion, which is native to North Africa but has not been seen

ALGERIA'S PROTECTED AREAS

Algeria's 11 national parks include coastal parks, mountain parks, Saharan parks, and one steppe park. Parc National d'El Kala (El Tarf), Parc National de Gouraya (Bejaïa), and Parc National de Taza (Jijel) are Algeria's coastal parks. The parks of the mountain areas are Parc National de Théniet El Had (Tissemsilt), Parc National du Djurdjura (Tizi Ouzou and Bouira), Parc National de Chréa (Blida), Parc National de Belezma (Batna), and Parc National de Tlemcen (Tlemcen). Parc National de Djebel Aissa (Naama) is the only park on the steppe. There are two parks of the Sahara. One, Parc National du Tassili, is in Illizi; the other, Parc National de l'Ahaggar, is in Tamanrasset.

Six of these parks are also biosphere reserves: Parc National de Chréa, Parc National d'El Kala, Parc National du Djurdjura, Parc National du Tassili, Parc National de Gouraya, and Parc National de Taza.

Nature reserves can be found at Oran and Mascara; M'sila; Guelma; Sétif; and Oran. They are Réserve Naturelle de la Macta; Réserve Naturelle de Mergueb; Réserve Naturelle des Beni-salah; Réserve Naturelle des Babors; and Réserve Naturelle Marine des Iles Habibas respectively. Some of Algeria's numerous wetland sites can be found at Skikda, Oran, Sétif, Naama, and Ghardaia. The Barcelona Convention's Specially Protected Areas of Mediterranean Interest are Réserve Marine du Banc des Kabyles (Jijel) and Réserve Naturelle Marine des Iles Habibas (Oran).

in the wild since 1922. IFAW, on the other hand, seeks to improve the welfare of wild and domestic animals throughout the world by protecting wildlife habitats, reducing commercial exploitation of animals, and assisting animals in distress.

Algeria has taken a very active role in nature conservation. It has in place comprehensive environmental laws and a system of protected areas. Although no marine parks exist in Algeria, the government has the authority to close maritime areas to fishing. As a party to the Convention on Biological Diversity as well as the Ramsar Convention on protecting wetlands, Algeria has recently added 16 conservation sites, bringing the country's total number of Ramsar sites to 42. These wetlands, which include complexes of lagoons and salt lakes that are representative of Algerian wetlands, cover a surface area of about 7.2 million acres (2.9 million ha). These designated wetland areas are high in biodiversity. One of the sites, the Guerbes Sanhadja, represents more than 10 ecosystems alone. The threatened white-headed duck breeds in this site.

ALGERIANS

ALGERIANS ARE PRIMARILY of Arab, Berber, and mixed Arab-Berber descent. Their physical features reflect the considerable fusion of peoples that has gone into creating modern Algeria. Algerians have a wide range of physical traits and complexions. It would be difficult to distinguish ethnic affiliation sheerly by physical features; instead language is the primary way in which Algerians tell communities apart. Berbers and Arabs have traditionally lived peacefully together, sharing their faith in Islam but following and retaining their different traditions. The French population has fallen to less than 1 percent from approximately 10 percent in colonial times. Many other Europeans and almost all of the 150,000 Jews that had resided in Algeria left the country after independence. Today there is no active Jewish community, though a very small number of Jews continue to live in Algiers. Mass migration of Algerians to Europe has also occurred, with nearly 9.1 million people of Algerian descent estimated to be living there, chiefly in France. In 1996 it was recorded that 5.1 million people

The name Moor *comes from the Latin* Mauri, *the name for the Berber inhabitants of the old Roman province of Mauritania, the territory now covered by Morocco and part of Algeria.*

Opposite: **Three Algerian teenage friends smiling for the camera.**

Left: **Two Tuareg men converse in the desert. Unlike other Muslims, Tuareg men wear veils covering their faces, while the women expose their faces.**

of Algerian descent resided in France, of whom 4.3 million were Muslim.

ARABS

Although several characteristics determine whether a person is an Arab, *Arab* broadly refers to people who speak Arabic as their native language. In fact, native Arabic speakers make up an estimated 80 percent of the Algerian population. The great majority of Algerian Arabs are Sunni Muslims.

References to Arabs as nomads and camel herders in northern Arabia appear in Assyrian inscriptions of the ninth century B.C. The name was subsequently applied to all inhabitants of the Arabian Peninsula. From time to time Arab kingdoms arose on the fringes of the desert, but no great Arab empire emerged until Islam appeared in the seventh century A.D.

Almost half of all Algerian Arabs live in cities. Although traditional tribal life has nearly disappeared, tribal values and identity retain some importance, especially when linked to Islam. Descent from the clan of Prophet Muhammad or from one of the first Arab tribes to accept Islam still carries great prestige. Many villages and towns are home to prominent families with common links to tribal ancestors. Blood ties contribute to the formation of political factions.

MOORS

When the Arab armies swept across northern Africa in the seventh century, they found indigenous tribespeople called Berbers living in the northwestern corner of the continent. After the Arabs converted many of the Berbers to Islam early in the eighth century, the Berbers and the Arabs joined forces to conquer

Spain. There they intermarried with the Spanish. Their descendants came to be called Moors, a term that is now archaic. *Moors* generally referred to people of mixed ancestry who lived along the coast of northwest Africa and al-Andalus (the Iberian Peninsula, which comprises Spain and Portugal).

The Moors reached the height of their power in Spain. After the conquest of the Visigothic kingdom in 711 and a period of great disorder, the highly cultured Arab caliphate of Cordoba was formed. The caliphate lasted until 1031. Following its collapse, the Moors who controlled northwestern Africa crossed to Spain and took over.

After the battle of Las Navas de Tolosa in 1212, in which Alfonso VIII of Castile broke the Moorish hold over central Spain, the Moors still ruled the kingdom of Granada. Granada rose to a splendor rivaling that of the former caliphate of Cordoba. It was not until 1492 that this Moorish kingdom, weakened by internal discord, was shattered by the armies of Ferdinand and Isabella. The Moors were then expelled from Spain.

These types of relationships are less prevalent in cities; even there, however, leading families may seek to intermarry their children to preserve traditional bonds, and many urban families retain patronage ties to their villages.

BERBERS

The name *Berber* refers to the descendants of the pre-Arab populations of North Africa. The Berbers are a composite people, exhibiting a broad range of physical features, and the bond among various Berber groups is almost entirely a linguistic one. It is uncertain how the term *Berber* came about, as Berbers refer to themselves by a variant of the word *amazigh* (AH-ma-zay), which means "free man" not only in Algeria but in Morocco, Libya, Egypt, and other parts of North Africa as well. The term seems to

Opposite: **An Arab in a long robe that protects the clothes beneath from desert storms.**

have been derived from the Latin and Arabic variation of the Greek word for non-Greek, *barbaroi*, which is taken to mean "foreigners" and which is etymologically associated with the term "barbarian."

The origins of Berbers are not certain either. The genetically predominant ancestors of the Berbers appear to have come from East Africa, the Middle East, or both. It is clear that they speak variations of a single language, Berber, while many also have a strong sense of tribal affiliations to Berber peoples including the Kabyle of Algeria, the Riffians and Shluh of Morocco, and the Tuareg of the Sahara.

Although almost all Algerians in the country are Berber in origin, those who identify themselves as Berbers represent less than 20 percent of Algeria's population and live mostly in rural areas. Algeria's four main Berber groups—Kabyle, Shawiya, M'zabite, and Tuareg—are differentiated by dialect, culture, and where they live.

Berber speakers, who today number about 25 million, can be found distributed throughout Libya, Tunisia, Egypt, Mali, Niger, Algeria, Morocco, Mauritania, and Western Sahara. While some speculate that the Berber language is steadily retreating in favor of Arabic as Algeria becomes more homogenized, others suggest that the Berber language is attracting new interest as a national or subnational language. Certainly an interest in reviving the language is growing among Algerian Berbers in the diaspora.

The maintenance of the Berber language and the identity that it carries is tied in with social and cultural traits that conspicuously distinguish the Berbers from the surrounding Arabs. Despite great diversity, the Berbers

Berbers generally have no sense of belonging to a Berber people or a nation but have strong loyalties to village, clan, and tribe.

Two Berber women. Berber women generally have a higher status than Arab women.

generally are rural, either settled or nomadic, with an economy based on subsistence agriculture and animal husbandry. They are grouped territorially and governed in egalitarian districts run by councils, of which the head of each extended family is a member.

Berber tribes living in the mountainous areas in the north traditionally practice transhumance—moving up and down the mountains according to season to find the best pastures for their animals. While the bulk of the tribe moves with the herds, a small group stays behind to guard the collective granaries and grow some essential grains and vegetables.

Under French rule many Berbers, especially Kabyles, became part of the French-speaking elite who dominated Algerian politics and finance. The French, in a "divide and rule" policy, deliberately favored the Kabyles in education and employment. As a result, in the years after independence Kabyles moved into all levels of state administration across Algeria, where they remained a large and influential group.

KABYLES The Kabyles, the largest Berber-speaking tribe in Africa, occupy the mountainous coastal area of Kabylia, in northern Algeria. They number approximately six million and are most resistant to

Girls playing in the Kabylia countryside.

national government intrusion. They were also the dominant group that demanded the Algerian government recognize Tamazight as a national language. Their historical origins, like those of other Berber peoples, are vague. Principally agriculturalists who cultivate cereal grains and olives, Kabyles also maintain their subsistence economy through goat herding. Villages of stone or chopped straw and clay are built on barren ridges or slopes overlooking gardens, orchards, and pastures. Many Kabyles have migrated to coastal cities or to France in search of employment, but they tend to stay together in clans.

Patrilineal clans characterize the marriage-family structure, with the husband's mother occupying a dominant position in the household. Councils composed of male elders govern each village, drawing upon a well-developed legal code to deal with property disputes and other offenses. Islam is the dominant religion, although some practice Christianity. Among rural populations, traditional beliefs in invisible beings and mysterious powers still persist. Although Kabyle women were traditionally restricted to the home, since Algeria gained independence their status has improved in terms of education and careers.

"Follow the path of your father and grandfather" is an old Kabyle saying adhered to even today.

SHAWIYAS   The Shawiyas have lived in the Aurès Mountains of eastern Algeria since the first wave of Arab invasions. Through the centuries Shawiyas remained largely isolated, farming among themselves in the north or following herds in the south. Only Kabyle peddlers or desert camel herders visited Shawiya villages. During the revolution the French herded many anti-French Shawiyas into concentration camps, disturbing the seclusion that had lasted for centuries.

M'ZABITES   Descendants of the Kharijite refugees who fled the Fatimids, the M'zabites live behind five walled cities along the northern Sahara near Wadi M'zab, which lent its name to the group. The M'zabites, like the Shawiyas, isolate themselves from the rest of the world. They call themselves "God's family." M'zabites follow a strict form of Islam and abide by their religious government of elders. M'zabite Islam provides social equality and literacy for men and women. However, women are not allowed to leave the oasis villages. Only M'zabite men can seek employment outside their village as merchants. By the mid-1980s M'zabites had built a retail trade that extended to Algiers, where they dominate the grocery and butchery business. A number of M'zabites now live in Algiers. No matter where M'zabites live, however, they always return to the desert.

TUAREGS   The Tuaregs are the most independent of the Berber groups. Their name is derived from the Arabic Badawi word *twareq*, the collective

A group of Shawiya men. Shawiya men believe their women have special magical powers. This belief gives Shawiya women slightly more privileges than Kabyle women.

65

The Tuaregs have had to modify their lifestyle in the face of government restrictions.

term for *tereq*, meaning "of God forsaken." It was used by the Arab bedouin who were frustrated by the Tuaregs' unwillingness to practice Islam. The Tuaregs' freewheeling desert culture, dominated by women, is regarded as an oddity. Legend has it that a Berber princess from Morocco journeyed across the severe desert with only her slave girl as companion. For her courage she was made leader of the Tuaregs—the first of a long line of female rulers. Tuareg women control the economy and property, and both boys and girls study the Koran. Through the years Tuareg men, but not women, wore veils. The custom proved practical as protection against sandstorms in the days when men roamed the Sahara on camels leading salt, gold, and date caravans.

Tuaregs traditionally range the Sahara through southern Algeria to northern Nigeria and from western Libya to Mali. Since the establishment of modern countries with firmly drawn borders, their traditional nomadic life has been severely restricted. The governments of Algeria and Niger, in particular, have limited the number of camel caravans allowed to pass the border each year. As a result, many Tuaregs moved south into Niger and Mali, but their numbers were depleted in the 1970s by disastrous droughts. Those who remained became seminomadic or even sedentary, tending their gardens around desert oases such as Tamanrasset and Djanet. Some Tuaregs have found a new livelihood transporting illegal immigrants across the Sahara. They help sub-Saharan Africans who seek entry into Europe

YVES SAINT LAURENT

Born in Oran on August 1, 1936, Yves Saint Laurent is a French fashion designer who furthered the trend for ready-to-wear clothes with his boutiques in Europe and the United States. The son of a successful French lawyer, he stayed in Algeria long enough to complete secondary school.

Saint Laurent left for Paris to pursue a career designing women's clothes and costumes for the theater. After a *Vogue* magazine executive showed designer Christian Dior some of Saint Laurent's sketches in 1954, Dior hired him immediately as his assistant. Upon Dior's death in 1957, Saint Laurent was chosen as head designer for the Dior establishment at the age of 21.

After induction into the French army and a subsequent nervous collapse, Saint Laurent opened his own Parisian fashion house in 1962. In 1966 he opened a series of boutiques that sold ready-to-wear designs. He also marketed perfume and accessories. He was responsible for popularizing pants for women for all occasions.

In 1983 the Metropolitan Museum of Art in New York held a retrospective covering 25 years of Saint Laurent's work. Saint Laurent is no longer active as a fashion designer, having retired in 1998, and he now spends much of his time in his home in Marrakesh, Morocco.

and need assistance to travel across the Sahara and the Mediterranean. Today some Tuaregs even work in Saharan gas and oil fields. Tuaregs currently number anywhere from 100,000 to 3.5 million.

PIEDS-NOIRS

When Algeria was a department of France, many French families lived in Algeria. Those of French origin who were born in Algeria were called *pieds-noirs* (pee-AY NWAH), literally meaning "black feet," because the early French troops wore high black boots. Although many of them lived most of their lives in Algeria, they considered themselves to be French and identified with France.

During the time of independence there were about one million expatriates in Algeria. As non-Muslims, this group had French citizenship. The non-Muslims felt more a part of European than Arab culture, and they fled Algeria in droves once the country gained independence. By the early 1980s there were only about 117,000 expatriates left in Algeria, of whom 75,000 were European, including 45,000 French. Today Europeans in Algeria account for less than 1 percent of the population.

LIFESTYLE

ALGERIA INCLUDES WITHIN ITS borders many distinct lifestyles. These range from that of the urban middle class, whose lifestyle differs from that of their European counterparts principally in their religious practices, to that of the nomads of the Sahara, whose lives follow a traditionally defined pattern quite foreign to most Westerners. Between these two extremes are the Berber villagers who constitute the bulk of Algerian society.

Fundamentally Berber in cultural and racial terms before the arrival of the Arabs and later the French, Algerian society was organized around the extended family, clan, and tribe and was adapted to a rural rather than an urban setting. In the villages, family and Islamic tradition continue to determine most aspects of people's lives. Agriculture remains the focus of economic activity.

In recent years, however, the lifestyles of Algerians were disrupted by the civil war that ravaged the country. Prominent public figures, intellectuals, journalists, and ordinary civilians were the target of attacks by Islamic militants. Certain towns and entire neighborhoods in some cities were virtually controlled by militants. Algerians who followed a less strict form of Islam were pressured to change their behavior under threat of death. Women and intellectuals were the most directly affected by Islamic pressure, but its effects were felt by all.

In the aftermath of the war, Algeria faces new challenges in combating residual militant Islamic groups and reconciling the tension between the

Above: **A Berber mother and daughters picking olives. For most people in the rural areas, family is the most important part of life.**

Opposite: **Algerians resting and chatting in Salah Oasis.**

69

promotion of Islam and Arab culture and the diversity that makes up modern Algeria. It also has to cope with rapid urbanization that puts a strain on not only housing and employment but also the family unit. Because of a severe housing shortage and a lack of employment opportunities, some Algerians choose to migrate in search of a better life. The falling fertility rates in Algeria may eventually mean smaller families, though for now many people in urban areas are cramped in small houses they share with their extended families.

PREINDEPENDENCE ALGERIA

Before the French occupation in 1830, Algerians were divided among a few ancient cities and a sparsely settled countryside where subsistence farmers and nomadic herdsmen lived in small tribes. In the cities most people identified themselves by their ethnic or religious group rather than by their class or economic standing. Social organization in the rural areas depended primarily on kinship ties. Essentially the social organization of rural Algerians was dependent on patrilineal family ties. At the basic level, a small kinship unit called an *ayla* (ai-la) was formed based on descent through a common grandfather or great-grandfather. Larger kinship groups, or clans, were known as *adhrum* by the Kabyles or *firq* by the Arabs.

Nomads in the Sahara follow a traditional lifestyle.

These clans consisted of a few *aylas* whose members were related by a more remote male relative. A tribe was formed when these clans came together, largely out of circumstance rather than familial or political loyalties. Only when their sovereignty was threatened did the Algerians accept the authority and advice of their tribal leader.

Settled Berber groups were democratic and egalitarian. They were governed by a council composed of adult males. Berber villages were not organized according to social standing and prestige.

French rule brought enormous social changes. Europeans took over the economic and political life of the country but remained socially aloof. Algerian urban merchants and artisans were squeezed out, and country landowners were dispossessed.

A rapid increase in population created tremendous pressure on agricultural lands. Villagers and tribespeople flocked to the towns and the cities, where they formed an unskilled labor mass, scorned by Europeans and isolated from the clans that had given them security and a sense of solidarity.

This urban movement increased after World War I, and after World War II large numbers migrated to France in search of work. The Kabyles were the principal migrants; during the 1950s as many as 10 percent of the people of Kabylia were working in France at any one time, and even larger numbers were working in cities of the Tell.

Nomadic clans were not spared from the social upheaval. Clans with few flocks and scant territory soon changed to a more sedentary lifestyle, settling along the outskirts of towns. They gradually assimilated with these communities and even adopted the traditional ancestors or saints of the townspeople.

THE REVOLUTION AND SOCIAL CHANGE

The war of independence resulted in dramatic social changes. The roles that many Algerians undertook in the war were instrumental in their forming new ideas and perceptions about themselves and their abilities. With newfound confidence, many young Algerians struck out on their own, creating a new class of leaders in the process.

The eight-year war, stretching across most of the country, emptied many rural villages. In addition, almost three million villagers were resettled by the French in what was called a regroupment program. Several of the program's camps became permanent settlements. Members of the rural villages were resettled into housing provided by the French. These new settlements, however, were not constructed with the traditional household in mind but instead catered to the nuclear family. As a result, many Algerians lost ties with their larger social groups and with their land.

A MUDDLED TRANSITION

The mid-1980s was a difficult time for Algerians, especially the young. Many found themselves torn between the lure of modernism and loyalty to tradition, between secularism and religion, and between individualism and community. Unemployment soared during this time and caused widespread apathy, frustration, and disillusionment among Algerian youths.

Algerians also faced a cultural identity problem. Because colonialism had altered precolonial institutions and values, the country was faced with the task of building a new national identity.

The government implemented a national "cultural revolution" to mold an Algerian identity and personality. It aimed to recover and

During Algeria's war of independence, Algerian women who were accustomed to a sheltered and segregated life found themselves suddenly thrust into revolutionary militancy.

FAMILY PLANNING

In the 20 years following independence, Algeria's population doubled. The average Algerian woman had between seven and nine children. With 3.2 percent population growth each year, Algeria was one of the world's faster-growing nations. There was concern that the country's economic growth would be hampered, as food, housing, and jobs were already limited.

The need for Algeria to implement a family-planning program slowly became evident. By the mid-1980s the government's efforts began to bear fruit. There was an overwhelming demand for information on family planning in some areas, so much so that it outweighed the supply. It was estimated that approximately 35 percent of Algerian women of childbearing age were using contraceptives. Meanwhile, the government continued to promote the importance of family planning and the use of contraceptives. As of 2000, 50 percent of Algerian women used contraceptives. Today Algeria's population growth rate has fallen to 1.22 percent.

popularize the past, to Arabize the country through such measures as the substitution of Arabic for French, and in general to create a distinctive national personality with which the country as a whole could identify. Progress was modest at best because of the lack of funding. Enthusiasm for it was also lukewarm, particularly among the Kabyle Berbers, who sought to preserve their cultural and linguistic distinctiveness.

During the past few years the Berbers have been very vocal in what they see as government repression of their culture while giving special status to Islam and Arab culture. In 2001 the Berbers finally won the acknowledgment they sought when the government recognized Tamazight, the Berber tongue, as a national language. Today Algeria recognizes aspects of Islam and both Arab and Berber ethnic identity as essential elements of its national identity. However, Algeria still struggles with the problem of unemployment, as it did in the 1980s. As the country becomes increasingly urbanized, lifestyles differ to reflect that change, and young adults seek opportunities such as employment that they feel should be available to them now that the civil war is over and the economy is on the mend.

Algeria absorbed the heaviest impact of all Arab countries subject to European rule.

FAMILY AND HOUSEHOLD

Before Algeria's independence, the rural family unit in particular consisted of the extended family. The senior male member exercised undisputed

A Tuareg family spending a leisure moment together. The traditional extended family consisted of grandparents, their married sons and families, unmarried sons, daughters if unmarried or divorced or widowed with their children in tow, and occasionally other related adults.

authority. Even after marriage, couples continued living with the groom's family. They cooked their own meals and lived in their own rooms that opened out onto the communal family courtyard. The entire family was involved in the raising of children, instilling in them the notion of group solidarity.

In recent years, particularly since independence, there has been a trend toward nuclear-family units. Families break away when the head of the extended family passes away. Alternatively, young married couples with the financial means to set up their own households often opt to do so. This trend is evident in urban areas, especially among the young and better educated. Birthrates have also declined, from an average of seven or eight children per woman in the 1960s and 1970s to an estimated average of 1.86 children per woman in 2007. In addition, in both urban and rural settings, there has been a developing tendency for wives to leave the household to perform labor seasonally or for a longer period.

HEALTH

In 1974 a system of virtually free national health care was introduced. Hospitalization, medicines, and outpatient care were free to all, the cost borne equally by the state and social security. In 1984 the government adopted a plan to transform the health sector from a curative system to a preventive one more suitable to the needs of a young population. Rather than investing in expensive hospitals, the government favored health centers and clinics along with vaccination programs. It was hoped that the infant mortality rate could be cut in half. The program was a success, with Algeria's infant mortality rates falling from 69 deaths per 1,000 live births in the 1990s to an estimated 28.78 deaths per 1,000 live births in 2007.

Tuberculosis, trachoma, hepatitis A, and typhoid remain among the most serious diseases today; gastrointestinal complaints, measles, and cholera, often brought about by inadequate sanitation facilities and a lack of safe drinking water, are relatively common as well. Tuberculosis is considered to be the most serious health hazard, infecting 54 and killing two out of every 100,000 of the total population. Trachoma, a fly-borne eye infection that is directly or indirectly responsible for most of the numerous cases of blindness in Algeria, is also a serious health concern. Malaria and poliomyelitis, both formerly endemic, have been brought under control.

In an effort to extend health care to everyone, the government requires all newly qualified physicians, dentists, and pharmacists to work in the public health service for at least five years. However, most of the medical personnel and facilities are concentrated in the north, while remote mountain locations and much of the Sahara do not have easy access to medical care.

The average lifespan of an Algerian was estimated to be 74 years in 2007.

Algerian men make most major decisions involving money, property, and contact with outsiders.

The moustache is a traditional symbol of manhood in Algeria, and to curse someone's moustache is one of the worst possible insults.

MEN AND WOMEN

Roles for men and women are well defined in Algerian society. The responsibility of maintaining the family's honor rests mainly upon the shoulders of the women in the family, particularly the sisters and the daughters. Any misconduct or impropriety, especially if publicly known, would be detrimental to the family's honor and result in the offending women being punished by the men in the family. As such, women are expected to be decorous, modest, and circumspect.

After marriage the bride usually leaves her family and goes to live with her husband's family, where she is under the scrutiny of her mother-in-law. The difficult relationship between mother-in-law and daughter-in-law leads to much tension, which is the cause of much marital friction.

The relationship between mother and son is often warm and close, while the son's relationship with his father is more distant. A woman gains status in the family when she bears sons. Mothers tend to nurse their sons for longer and love and favor them more than their daughters.

Many Algerian women today are under considerable social pressure to use the veil as part of their dress code. This usually means wearing the *hijab* (HEE-juub), a headscarf covering their hair, ears, and neck but not their face. This practice has increased, particularly during the past 15 years, due to the influence of religious extremist groups and attacks on unveiled women. In remote or conservative rural areas such as the south, women are often seen covered from head to toe, exposing only their eyes. However, it is rare to see women working in government offices dressed in that manner, although they do cover their heads and hair.

ACTIVISTS AND WOMEN'S RIGHTS UNDER ATTACK

Nabila Djahnine, an architect who led an organization called Tighri n Tmettut ("Cry of Women" in Berber), was gunned down on February 15, 1995, at the age of 35 by two men in a car as she walked to work. It is believed that Islamic militants were behind the murder.

Djahnine, a well-known activist in Tizi-Ouzou since she was a student, had helped to start a magazine called *Voice of Women* in 1990. In her writing she defended Algerian women's right to participate in the civil and political life of their country. Despite escalating attacks on activists known for their opposition to the agenda of the armed Islamist militants, Djahnine remained an outspoken advocate for women's rights. Djahnine's organization, like so many of Algeria's other, numerous small women's-rights groups, has called for the elimination of discriminatory provisions from Algeria's family code, although no amendments have yet been made.

The cancellation of parliamentary elections in 1992 led to fighting between the Algerian government and the armed Islamic opposition. Women were increasingly the targets of such violence. Women who worked outside the home were threatened and killed by Islamic militants. The headscarf came to be seen as a powerful symbol by those vying for power. Because of this, Algerian women were killed by Islamic militants for refusing to wear the veil or by the militants' opponents for agreeing to wear the veil. Other women were threatened with death because of their own or their family members' identification with the government or the security forces. Algerian defenders of women's rights believed that the armed Islamic groups targeted women as important cultural symbols: By driving women from the streets, the Islamic militants demonstrated their power to impose the culture they envisioned for Algeria. Between 1995 and 1998, women's-rights activists estimated, some 5,000 women were assaulted.

Even after the civil war, Algerian women continue to face discrimination due to a lack of government legislation prohibiting violence against women. The government has also failed to investigate and bring to justice those who had committed violence against women during the 11-year Algerian conflict. Women are now more vocal in asserting their rights, as seen by the rise of small women's-rights organizations. One such group is the National Women's Committee, an offshoot of the General Union of Algerian Workers (UGTA), which now has 130,000 members campaigning against sexual harassment in the workplace.

The greatest battle for women's rights was fought over the family code that was enacted in 1984 specifying the laws relating to familial relations. For years the government tried to advance the legal status of women, but Muslim fundamentalists saw any changes as moves to westernize Algerian family life. President Bendjedid put aside the first draft of the code in 1982 because of opposition from vocal women's groups, yet two years later a more conservative version was passed without debate. In 2004 President Bouteflika announced that amendments would be made to the code, but changes have yet to be drafted. Although women gained rights to child custody and their dowries, the code guaranteed men's access to unilateral divorce and their right to determine whether women could work outside the home.

Women in Algeria have made some progress in society. They can vote and run for office, and the number of female wage earners has increased considerably since Algeria's independence. Some moderate Islamic leaders have publicly defended the right of women to work. Women currently make up about 31 percent of the Algerian workforce. Many of them are highly educated, trained, and employed in medicine, education, and the media, and some women even serve in the armed forces. Algerian women are well represented in the judiciary—34 percent of magistrates are women. Women are also represented in parliament where, through an informal arrangement, opposition parties reserve 20 percent of their electoral lists for female candidates. In the 2002 elections women gained 24 out of 389 seats in the National People's Assembly. In 2004 a female politician, Louisa Hanoune, even ran for president, although she was unsuccessful.

MARRIAGE

Traditionally marriage was proposed to strengthen existing family ties rather than to expand the family. Because the sexes did not ordinarily mix socially, young men and women had few or no acquaintances among the opposite sex. Parents arranged marriages for their children, finding a mate through their own contacts or a professional matchmaker. Today romantic love is not uncommon, and Algerian men and women are free to marry whomever they wish as long as their marriage partner is approved by the family. Typically an Algerian man will express his interest in a particular woman to his mother. She then considers the match after looking into the suitability of the woman and her family. If she is deemed acceptable, the groom-to-be's family approaches the woman's family to propose the union. A date will then be chosen for the engagement.

An Islamic marriage is a civil contract rather than a sacrament. Representatives from the bride's and the bridegroom's sides meet to negotiate the terms of the marriage and the repercussions if the union is broken. Even though the couple must consent to the union by law, they are usually not included in the arrangements.

Opposite: **The French colonialists opposed veiling. In reaction, Algerians increased its use after independence. Paradoxically, however, this also resulted from the greater freedom enjoyed by women. The purpose of the veil was to provide mobile seclusion, and more frequent entry of women into public situations was made possible by the veil.**

DRESS

Algerian clothing is a blend of Western style and Islamic custom, especially in cities.

Traditional dress for rural women and girls involves draping a long piece of cloth over the entire body into a *haik* (HA-egg). Worn on the head to hide the lower part of the face, the *haik* also covers the clothes underneath. In addition, many rural women hang charms around their neck to ward off the "evil eye" that brings bad luck. Traditional Berber dress varies from region to region but generally consists of long skirts, blouses, and shawls with floral patterns, stripes, or embroidery in bright colors. Dresses also come in a variety of colors, although red, green, and brown are favored. In the eastern part of Algeria, dark-colored dresses are common, while in the western and central regions, white is favored. In cities, younger women wear Western dress. As a compromise, some religious yet urban women wear a veil covering their hair and sometimes even their lower face.

Most men and boys in cities wear variations of Western-style clothing. They have shirts, jackets, and either Western-style or fuller pants. Some businessmen wear suits and maybe a fez—a felt hat worn by North African Muslim men. In villages, men can be seen in a long hooded robe called a burnoose, made of linen for summer and wool for winter. Tuareg men wrap five yards of indigo material around the head into a turban that also goes over their robes, hiding all but their eyes.

A couple in traditional Berber dress. Berber women do not wear the veil.

HOUSING

The need for housing has been a pressing problem for the Algerian government for several decades. It was especially bad during the latter half of the 20th century, when shantytowns proliferated in and around cities owing to the constant influx of the population from rural to urban areas. After Algeria gained its independence, many Europeans left so quickly that they simply abandoned their houses. Squatters from the countryside then moved in, cramming as many as six families into a single house. It was only in the mid-1980s that the government made an effort to relieve urban housing shortages.

The government in 1972 undertook a rural public-housing project named the One Thousand Socialist Villages. This was planned to curb the continual flow of people to the cities. The plan was to construct villages, complete with schools and medical facilities, with the capacity to accommodate as many as 1,500 people. Each housing unit had three rooms and was equipped with heat, electricity, and running water. Even though 120 villages had been completed by mid-1979, migration to urban areas had not been curbed.

In the mid-1980s the urbanscape had changed from modern buildings of glass and concrete to crowded shantytowns. As more rural people migrated to urban areas, entire rural settlements called *gourbis* (GOHR-bi) sprouted up in coastal cities such as Annaba. *Gourbis* were dwellings created out of mud and branches or sometimes stone and clay. The roofs were usually flat, but in certain

A modern urban apartment complex.

parts of eastern Algeria that are subject to heavy rain and snowfall, the roofs were steeply slanted to allow for runoff.

During the early postindependence years, Kabylia was the only area to experience a housing boom. Many Berbers from Kabylia had families living and working in France who provided them with the finances necessary to construct in Kabylia.

Algeria has a large cash reserve from its petroleum-based economy, but the problems of inadequate housing and unreliable water and electrical supply are not being addressed quickly enough. According to the United Nations Development Program, Algeria has one of the world's highest per-housing-unit occupancy rates. In addition, the country has an immediate shortfall of 1.5 million housing units. In 1998 a loan of $150 million was offered by the World Bank to help Algeria eliminate the problem of urban slums. This 10-year program aims to help improve and create low-income urban housing for the masses. Algeria's construction sector also benefited from loans from the European Union and from other Arab countries.

EDUCATION

Before independence, Algeria's education system was European oriented, and lessons were taught entirely in French. French and Algerian schoolchildren were segregated, and fewer than one-third of Muslim school-age children were enrolled in primary school. Only 30 percent and 10 percent of students at secondary and tertiary levels respectively were Algerian.

Subsequently Algeria's education underwent major changes, and French and Algerian children were desegregated. Under the 1954 Constantine Plan for the improvement of Muslim living conditions, increases in Muslim enrollments in schools were scheduled.

The government sought to create an education system that was better suited to the needs of the developing nation. It aimed to increase literacy, provide free education, institute mandatory primary education, replace all foreign teachers, and make Arabic the language of instruction. Children started their compulsory basic education at the age of six. Primary and secondary education was reorganized into a nine-year course. Following that, students went down a general, technical, or vocational track before sitting for a baccalaureate examination for entry into a university, a state technical institute, or a vocational training center. By the early 1980s attendance approached 90 percent in urban centers and 67 percent in rural areas. Although education is free and officially compulsory, enrollment usually falls short of 100 percent. Currently 97 percent of boys and 91 percent of girls attend school in Algeria. Teachers are nearly all Algerian, and instruction is officially entirely in Arabic, French being introduced only in the third year. In 2003 Berber was included as part of the language of instruction; prior to that, teachers used to punish children who uttered Berber in the schoolyard. The study of Islam was also made compulsory as part of the school curriculum.

Students at a school in Algeria.

About 6 percent of Algeria's GDP is spent on education, with a bulk of the money going to teacher training, technical and scientific programs, and adult literacy classes. The Ministry of Education and the Ministry of Religious Affairs jointly regulate public schools.

RELIGION

ALMOST ALL ALGERIANS are Muslim. Though the constitution declares Islam to be the state religion, it prohibits discrimination based on religious belief. The government protects the rights of the small Christian and Jewish populations and often includes leaders of these communities at ceremonial state functions.

There is no active Jewish community in Algeria today, and Jews number fewer than 100. When armed Islamic groups threatened to eliminate Jews during the civil conflict, many Jews left Algeria for France and Israel, abandoning the single remaining synagogue in Algiers. Since the departure of the French, Christianity has become a peripheral religion. Algerian Christians reportedly number fewer than 11,000 and often worship only in private. For security reasons, largely due to the civil conflict, Roman Catholic and Protestant churches are found mainly in large cities such as Algiers, Annaba, and Oran. Conversion from Islam to Christianity is extremely rare and is frowned upon by the Muslim community. Consequently Algerians who convert from Islam do so clandestinely.

The relationship between religion and state has always been close in Algeria. The Islamic clergy receives religious training administered by the government, and the Ministry of Religious Affairs appoints imams (Muslim religious leaders) to both state and privately funded mosques. On at least three occasions in 1993, progovernment imams were assassinated.

Above: **Three elderly Algerian Muslim men resting outside the entrance to a mosque.**

Opposite: **Algerian Muslims pray in the Kawtar Mosque in Blida, Algiers, during the holy month of Ramadan.**

During that same year, several imams were reportedly removed from their positions for preaching antigovernment views. More recently the government has punished a number of imams for inflammatory sermons following the May 2003 earthquake. Friday sermons at larger mosques are reportedly monitored by security forces, leading regime critics to argue that their freedom of religion has been compromised.

BASIC TENETS OF ISLAM

Islam means "submission to God" (Allah), and those who submit to Allah are known as Muslims. The fundamental belief of Muslims as stated by the *shahadah* (SHAR-HAR-dah), the Islamic testimony of faith, is that "there is no god but God (Allah) and Muhammad is his Prophet." Muslims repeat this testimony sincerely during many rituals. The revelations made by Muhammad, the "seal of prophets," is considered to bring to completion the series of biblical revelations received by Jews and Christians. It is thought that people had deviated from the true teachings of Allah until Muhammad came to set things right.

Islam stands on five pillars: to witness that there is no God but Allah and that Muhammad is his Prophet; to perform the required prayers; to pay the *zakat* (ZAHR-cut), or charity dues; to fast during the month of Ramadan; and to perform the pilgrimage to Mecca (hajj). Whenever possible, men pray in congregation at the mosque under an imam, and on Friday they are obliged to do so. Women may also attend public worship at the mosque, where they are segregated from the men, although most frequently they pray in seclusion at home.

Initially almsgiving was imposed on people by means of taxing their wealth proportionately, with the taxes subsequently distributed to the needy and to mosques. Now such giving is left up to the individual.

In remembrance of Allah's revealing his word, the Koran, to Muhammad, Muslims partake in a month-long, obligatory fast. During Ramadan, the ninth month of the Muslim calendar, Muslims abstain from eating, drinking, smoking, and sexual intercourse during the day. Only those who are ill or otherwise exempt do not have to abstain.

All Muslims are expected to make the hajj, a pilgrimage to the holy city of Mecca, at least once in their lives to take part in the activities and rituals there. These activities are held during the 12th month of the lunar calendar.

A Muslim's first duty is to his or her immediate family.

SOCIAL RESPONSIBILITIES OF MUSLIMS

The teachings of Islam concerning social responsibilities are based on kindness to and consideration of others. Because a general injunction to be kind is likely to be ignored in certain situations, Islam lays emphasis on specific acts of kindness and defines the responsibilities and rights of various relationships. In a widening circle of relationship, the Muslims' first obligation is to their immediate family, then to other relatives, neighbors, friends and acquaintances, orphans and widows, the needy of the community, fellow Muslims, all humans, and animals.

Respecting and caring for parents is an important part of a Muslim's expression of faith. The Koran says, "Your Sustainer has decreed that you worship none but Him, and that you be kind to parents. Whether one or both of them attain old age in your lifetime, do not say to them a word of contempt nor repel them, but address them in terms of honor. And, out of kindness, lower to them the wing of humility and say: My Sustainer! Bestow on them Your mercy, even as they cherished me in childhood." Regarding the duty toward neighbors, Prophet Muhammad

HUMAN RIGHTS IN AN ISLAMIC STATE

THE SECURITY OF LIFE AND PROPERTY In the Prophet's address during his final pilgrimage, he said, "Your lives and properties are forbidden to one another till you meet your Lord on the Day of Resurrection." He also said, "One who kills a man under covenant [i.e., a non-Muslim citizen of a Muslim land] will not even smell the fragrance of Paradise."

THE PROTECTION OF HONOR The Koran does not allow one's personal honor to be abused: "O You who believe, do not let one set of people make fun of another set. Do not defame one another. Do not insult by using nicknames. Do not backbite or speak ill of one another."

SANCTITY AND SECURITY OF PRIVATE LIFE The Koran guarantees privacy: "Do not spy on one another and do not enter any houses unless you are sure of their occupant's consent."

SECURITY AND PERSONAL FREEDOM Islam prohibits the imprisonment of any individual before his guilt has been proven before a public court. This means that the accused has the right to defend himself and to expect fair and impartial treatment from the court.

FREEDOM OF EXPRESSION Islam allows freedom of thought and expression, provided that it does not involve spreading that which is harmful to individuals and the society at large. For example, the use of abusive or offensive language in the name of criticism is not allowed. In the days of the Prophet, Muslims used to ask him about certain matters. If he had received no revelation on that particular issue, they were free to express their personal opinions.

FREEDOM OF ASSOCIATION The formation of associations, parties, and organizations is allowed, on the understanding that they abide by certain general rules.

FREEDOM OF CONSCIENCE AND CONVICTION The Koran states: "There should be no coercion in the matter of faith." Totalitarian societies throughout the ages have tried to deprive individuals of their freedom by subordinating them to state authority. Islam forbids such practice. Along with freedom of conviction and freedom of conscience, Islam guarantees the individual that his religious sentiments will be given due respect and nothing will be said or done that may encroach upon this right.

THE RIGHT TO BASIC NECESSITIES OF LIFE Islam recognizes the right of the needy to demand help from those who are more fortunate: "And in their wealth there is acknowledged right for the needy and the destitute."

said, "He is not a believer who eats his fill when his neighbor beside him is hungry; and He does not believe whose neighbors are not safe from his injurious conduct."

Muslims have a moral responsibility not only to their parents, relatives, and neighbors but also to all other humans, to animals, and to useful trees and other plants. For example, hunting birds and other animals for the sake of game is not permitted. Similarly, cutting trees and plants that yield fruit is forbidden unless there is a very pressing need for it.

ISLAM AND THE ALGERIAN STATE

Algeria's relationship with Islam has been complex and turbulent. After independence, the socialist government vigorously suppressed any

A mass public prayer in Algeria. Religion has become a powerful force in contemporary Algeria.

Islamic activism throughout the 1960s and 1970s. Many government workers and other employees judiciously kept clean-shaven to avoid overt identification with Islamists. These actions of self-consciousness and self-censorship are perhaps consequences of socialism and a reminder of French colonial days.

Under President Boumédienne the government asserted state control over religious activities for the purpose of national consolidation and political control. This policy did not, however, mean any change in the standing of Islam as the state religion. Boumédienne insisted upon rigid observance of the holy month of Ramadan and its fast. Similarly, he discouraged production and consumption of wine and decreed a change in the weekend from Saturday/Sunday to Thursday/Friday, much to the dismay of government technocrats and the commercial classes. Although the Boumédienne regime consistently sought, to a far greater extent than its predecessor, to increase Islamic awareness and reduce Western influence, the rights of non-Muslims continued to be respected.

During the 1970s what may be termed an Islamic revival began, an outgrowth of popular disenchantment with industrialization, urbanization, and the problems of a developing society. Manifestations of the revived interest in Islam could be detected in increased mosque attendance; in requests for prayer rooms in factories, offices, and universities; and in a spectacular increase in pilgrimages to Mecca. The movement, which was especially strong among the young, enjoyed the support of Islamic fundamentalists and was responsible for a modification of the government's religious policies.

The Ministry of Religious Affairs continues to dominate the Algerian religious sphere, providing financial support and controlling all public mosques as well as supervising religious education. The ministry provided

MARABOUTS

Persons who were remarkable in one way or another and consequently were believed to have *baraka* (bah-RUCK-car), or special blessedness or grace, were called *marabouts* (MARE-rah-ba-outs). This special status could be acquired by temporal leaders who commanded the respect of their followers, performed acts of charity, and had a reputation for justness, or by spiritual leaders who had studied in Koranic schools, had admirable personal qualities, and could perform miracles. *Marabout* status could also be acquired by having *baraka* bestowed by a *marabout* or by dying heroically. *Marabouts* were North African holy men, frequently described by English-language writers as saints. They had no place in pristine Islam and were looked on with disfavor by the orthodox.

Brotherhoods of disciples frequently formed around particular *marabouts*, especially those who preached an original *tariqa* (TAR-ee-ka), a mystical or devotional "way." Each founder, an obvious possessor of great *baraka*, ruled an order of adepts who were ordinarily organized hierarchically. Before the 20th century, *marabouts* and their followers played significant political and moral roles, especially in western Algeria.

In the mid-1980s several of the *marabout* brotherhoods were still alive, although their membership had declined, and some had been abolished by government decree. Nonetheless, veneration of *marabouts* and other glorified leaders was common throughout the Maghrib, and some observers saw *marabout* leaders as having regained some influence in rural areas after Algeria gained independence. Shrines were established at the place of death of a leader or a *marabout* or at some place associated with an event in his life, and every village, city, or area of a city had its patron saint or saints who epitomized Muslim virtues and whose saintliness had been transformed into magical *baraka* at his special shrine. The influence of *marabouts* and brotherhoods has since declined, and none of the postindependence regimes have had any interest in their revival, because they represent fragmentation and disunity.

Many Algerians also accept the presence of mysterious powers and invisible beings. These might be benevolent or malevolent and must, as appropriate, be greeted, honored, propitiated, or avoided. Particularly in the countryside, Islam was mixed with a variety of pre-Islamic beliefs and practices. These included magic, various agricultural rites, and fear of the evil eye. (*Pictured here, a shrine at Timimoun.*)

Around A.D. 100, Romans banished Jews from Europe to North Africa. Many Berbers converted to Judaism.

guidance on sermons and sought to keep dissent out of mosques. In 2005 the Educational Commission was created within the ministry, composed of 28 members to develop a curriculum concerning the Koran. The commission was set up to provide guidelines for the hiring of teachers for Koranic schools and to ensure that imams are of the highest educational caliber. This was much different from the mid-1980s, when 60 percent of the 5,000 practicing imams paid by the state possessed inadequate training, with some of them actually illiterate. The commission also works in line with government guidelines to stem Islamic fanaticism.

THE PEOPLE OF THE BOOK

The Prophet enjoined his followers to convert the infidel to the true faith. He specifically exempted, however, the People of the Book—Jews and Christians, whose religions he recognized as the historical basis of Islam. These peoples were to be permitted to continue their own communal and religious life, as long as they recognized the temporal domain of Muslim authorities, paid their taxes, and did not proselytize or otherwise interfere with the practice of Islam.

Soon after arriving in Algeria the French Christian colonists tried to exert their religious and cultural dominance over the society. Yet the Islamic social order of Algeria assumed that Muslims would be the ruling powers; therefore, governance by France was interpreted as a cultural affront to Muslims, who rallied to resist French rule. Islam, in this way, played a role in Algerian nationalism.

At independence there were large Jewish and Christian communities. The Jewish community in Algeria was of considerable antiquity. Some members claimed descent from Palestinian immigrants in pre-Roman times and a majority from refugees from Spanish persecution early

SAINT AUGUSTINE OF HIPPO

Saint Augustine (354–430) was one of the foremost philosopher-theologians of early Christianity, and while serving as bishop of Hippo Regius (modern Annaba), he was the leading figure in the church of North Africa. He had a profound influence on the development of Western thought and culture and, more than any other person, shaped the themes and defined the problems that have characterized the Western tradition of Christian theology. Among his many writings considered classics, the two most celebrated are his semiautobiographical *Confessions* and *City of God*, a Christian vision of history.

Augustine was born at Thagaste (modern Souk Ahras), a small town in the Roman province of Numidia. The first part of Augustine's life can be seen as a series of attempts to reconcile his Christian faith with his Roman culture. His mother, Saint Monica, a Christian Berber, raised him as a Christian.

He received a classical education that schooled him in Latin literature. As a student in Carthage, he encountered the classical idea of philosophy's search for truth and was fired with enthusiasm for the philosophic life. Unable to give up Christianity altogether, however, he adopted Manichaeism, a Christian heresy claiming to provide a rational Christianity on the basis of a purified text of Scripture. Trained at Carthage in rhetoric (public oratory), he became a teacher of rhetoric in Carthage, Rome, and finally Milan.

In Milan he discovered, through a chance reading of some books of Neoplatonism, a form of philosophy that seemed compatible with Christian belief. At the same time, he found that he was finally able to give up the ambitions for public success that had previously prevented him from embracing the philosophic life. In 386, Augustine underwent religious conversion. He retired from his public position and received baptism from Ambrose, the bishop of Milan. With a small group of friends, he returned to North Africa and, in Thagaste, established a religious community dedicated to the intellectual quest for God.

Augustine's ordination, unexpectedly forced upon him by popular acclamation during a visit to Hippo in 391, brought about a fundamental change in his life and thought. He eventually succeeded in bringing together the philosophic Christianity of his youth and the popular Christianity of his congregation in Hippo.

His subsequent career as priest and bishop was to be dominated by controversy and debate. Especially important were his struggles with the Donatists and with Pelagianism. In both of these controversies, Augustine opposed forces that set some Christians apart from others on grounds of religious exclusivism or moral worth.

A small Christian shrine. Christianity came to Algeria very early in its history.

in the 15th century. They had numbered well in excess of 100,000 before the Algerian revolution, but at independence in 1962 nearly all of them departed. Because the Cremieux Decree of 1870 had granted them full French citizenship, most of the Jews went to France.

The government of independent Algeria discouraged anti-Semitism, and shortly after independence the small remaining Jewish population appeared to have stabilized at roughly 1,000 individuals, although the number is much lower today. The only remaining synagogue in Algiers was sacked by a group of youths in early 1977.

CHRISTIANITY

Christianity came to North Africa in the first or early second century. Its influence declined during the chaotic period of the Vandal invasions but was strengthened in the succeeding Byzantine period, only to be eliminated after the Arab invasions of the seventh century.

The Roman Catholic Church was introduced after the French conquest of Algeria. The diocese of Algiers was established in 1838. Proselytization of the Muslim population was at first strictly prohibited, and few conversions were accomplished at any time. The several Roman Catholic missions established in Algeria were concerned with charitable and relief work; the establishment of schools, workshops, and infirmaries; and the training of staff for the new establishments. Some of the missionaries of these organizations remained in the country after independence, working among the poorer segments of the population. There are also small communities of Seventh-Day Adventists and other Protestants. Because the government has adopted a policy of not inquiring about religious affiliations in censuses or surveys, the number of Christians in Algeria is not known, although estimates have placed it between 5,000 and 11,000.

A Catholic church in Oran, one of a few in Algeria.

LANGUAGE

LANGUAGE IS THE PRIMARY WAY Algerians tell ethnic communities apart. Before the Arab invasions, all groups spoke some form of Berber. Arabic encroached gradually, spreading through the areas most accessible to migrants and conquerors. In many rural areas, Berber remained the mother tongue. Later, when France took control of Algeria, French was made the first language. Algerians continued to speak Arabic and Berber in their homes as a form of protest.

Today Arabic is the official national language and the language of the majority of Algerians. Speaking and writing Arabic identifies Algerians with Islam, Arab culture, and other Arab countries. A modern form of Arabic, called modern literary Arabic or standard Arabic (MSA), is used for radio, television, theater, and public speaking.

Reorienting society to Arabic has been a slow process. The four main Berber groups continue to use their own languages, and French persists as a necessity for some businesses and in technical and scientific fields. Algeria has three radio networks broadcasting in Arabic, French, English, and Tamazight (the Berber language). French is still taught as a second language in schools because of its usefulness in an international setting. English is also taught as a foreign language in schools, although it is a very distant second in popularity after French.

Language has been a focal point of ethnic conflict in Algeria in recent years. Berber resistance to Arabization has focused on demands for recognition of Tamazight as an official language alongside Arabic. In 2002 this demand was acknowledged, and Tamazight took its place next to Arabic as one of Algeria's national languages.

Above: **A street sign is located in an unlikely spot—the middle of the desert.**

Opposite: **A newsstand displaying various newspapers in French and Arabic.**

97

BANQUE DE L'AGRICULTUE ET DU DEVELOPPEMENT RURAL

ARABIC AND BERBER

A Semitic tongue related to Hebrew, Aramaic, and Amharic, Arabic was introduced to the coastal regions of Algeria in the seventh and eighth centuries A.D. by Arab conquerors. The arrival of bedouin Arabs in the 11th century further deepened the influence of Arab language and culture.

Written Arabic is important as the vehicle of Islam and Arab culture and as a link with other Arab countries. Three forms are used today: the classical Arabic of the Koran, Algerian dialectical Arabic, and modern literary Arabic. The Arabic of the Koran is the essential base of written Arabic and the model of linguistic perfection, according to the beliefs of Islam. It is the vehicle of a vast religious, scientific, historical, and literary heritage. Arabic scholars and individuals with a good education from any country can converse with one another using classical Arabic.

In classical Arabic only the consonants are written; vowel signs and other marks to aid in pronunciation are employed only occasionally in printed

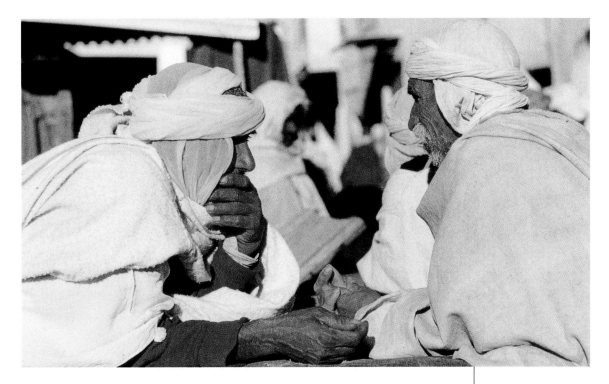

texts. The script is cursive, lending itself to use as decoration, and Arabic calligraphy is an important art form. It is written from right to left.

Literary Arabic, a simplified version of classical Arabic, is used in literature, the theater, newspapers, radio, and public speaking throughout the Middle East. A majority of Algerians, however, speak only dialectical Arabic. Even within Algerian Arabic there are significant local variations due to the influence of Berber, Turkish, and French loanwords.

Tamazight, the Berber language, is like Arabic a member of the Afro-Asiatic family of languages, variants of which are found throughout the Maghrib. Around 27.3 percent of Algerians speak Berber, mainly in the Kabylia, Batna, and Sahara regions. Berber is not so much a written language as an oral one. However, an ancient script called *tifinagh* (TEE-fee-nay) remains and is used among the Tuaregs of the Algerian Sahara for special purposes other than communication.

There has been considerable borrowing of words between Tamazight and Arabic. In some Arabic-speaking zones the names for various flora, fauna, and places are still in Tamazight.

Algerian men chatting. Several Berber dialect groups are recognizable in modern Algeria, but only the dialects of the Kabyle and Shawiya are spoken by any considerable number. The dialect of the Shawiya, which is distinguishable from but related to the Kabyle dialect, bears the mark and influence of Arabic. Separate dialects are spoken by the Tuareg and the M'zabite.

ARABIZATION

The French attempted to "civilize" Algeria by imposing French language and culture on it. As a result, education was oriented toward French, and advanced education in classical Arabic virtually ceased except among small numbers of religious scholars. Dialectical Arabic remained the language of everyday discourse for the vast majority of the population, but it was cut off from modern intellectual and technological developments and consequently failed to develop the flexibility and vocabulary needed for modern bureaucratic, financial, and intellectual affairs.

In reaction, the leaders of the revolution and successive governments committed themselves to Arabic as the national language. The aim was to recover the precolonial past and to use it to restore—if not to create—a national identity. The goal of Arabization is a country with its own language (Arabic), religion (Islam), and national identity (Algerian) free of French language and influence.

Beginning in the late 1960s the government of President Boumédienne decreed the first steps to promote literary Arabic in the bureaucracy and the schools. The problems inherent in this process of language planning immediately came to the fore. One of the most obvious was that for the overwhelming majority of Algerians, literary Arabic was quite foreign. There was also an almost total lack of qualified Arabic teachers. Other obstacles included widespread use of French in the state-run media and the continued preference for French as the working language of government and urban society. It soon became obvious to students that their prospects for gainful employment were bleak without facility in French, a fact that contributed to public skepticism regarding Arabization.

The problems that Algeria faces in Arabization are as evident today as they were several decades ago. French remains the language of the

business elite in Algeria, and it was therefore somewhat ironic that in early 2006 President Bouteflika ordered 42 private French-language schools in the country to be closed for not giving priority to the Arabic language. There is a growing concern that the continued lack of qualified Arabic teachers in Algeria will create a generation of students who will be incompetent in both French and Arabic.

There has also been opposition to Arabization from the Berbers. Young Kabyle students were particularly vocal in expressing their opposition. In the early 1980s their movement and demands formed the basis of the so-called Berber Question, also known as the Kabyle cultural movement. Although Tamazight is recognized as one of Algeria's national languages, it is not a compulsory subject in school. The teaching of the language also lacks standardization in addition to suffering from a shortage of qualified teachers.

Kabyle militants of the 1980s vigorously opposed Arabization of the educational system and the government bureaucracy and the adoption of literary Arabic as Algeria's official language. The banner on the right depicts *tifinagh*, an ancient Berber script.

THE RISKY PROFESSION OF JOURNALISM

All newspapers, book publishing, and broadcasting activities are under the control of the central government. Some of the main Arabic language dailies are El Youm, Ech-Chaab, *and* El Massa. *French-language dailies include* El Moudjahid, El Watan, Liberté, *and* La Tribune. *There are three English-language newspapers published in the country,* Algiers Post, All Headline News, *and* El Khabar. El Khabar *is also published in Arabic and French.*

On October 18, 1993, Smail Yefseh, a television journalist, was stabbed twice in the back and then shot in the chest and the stomach. It was 8:00 A.M., and dozens of passersby watched as three well-dressed young men fatally assaulted Yefseh.

Yefseh was the seventh of more than 50 Algerian journalists assassinated between 1993 and 1997. Many had their throats slashed or were shot at close range in front of their families.

Some 150,000 to 200,000 Algerians died in the civil war that started when the country's first free parliamentary elections were nullified in January 1992. Although other professions suffered greater losses than the press, the number of media members killed represents a high proportion of the approximately 500 journalists working in Algeria. The killing of journalists symbolized the freedom of speech lost by Algerians because of the war. Islamic militants were largely blamed for the attacks on journalists, but many local journalists also suspected the state's involvement in some of the killings. Their suspicions were intensified when the government kept its investigations of the killings closed and forbade independent international inquiries.

Although the civil war has since ended, journalists in Algeria still live in fear of government reprisal in the form of defamation suits and criminal charges. Like journalists a decade ago, journalists today do not enjoy freedom of the press. In 2001 the government enacted amendments to the penal code stiffening punishments for verbal attacks on public officials. Offenders can also be fined and imprisoned for up to 12 months for words or images deemed insulting toward the president, the justice system, the army, or any other state body or public institution.

NAMES

For those familiar with the European tradition of using a first name, an optional middle name, and a last name, names in the Arab world can seem perplexing, not least because they can run to enormous length. However, there is a logical structure to the Arab naming convention that, once seen, makes it simple to decipher a person's recent ancestry.

Suppose a man's name is Ali bin Ahmed bin Saleh Al-Fulani. He is called Ali by his friends and family. His family name is Al-Fulani. *Bin* (been) means "son of" (as does *ibn*), so *bin Ahmed bin Saleh* means that he is the son of Ahmed who is in turn the son of Saleh. Many Arabs can give their paternal ancestors' names for at least five or six generations, if not more.

What about women's names? Ali's sister is named Nura bint Ahmed bin Saleh Al-Fulani. *Bint* (bee-nt) means "daughter of." Thus her name means "Nura, the daughter of Ahmed who is the son of Saleh." So we have her given name, her father's name, her grandfather's name, and the family name.

It is interesting to note that when an Arab woman marries she does not change her name. When the above-mentioned Nura marries, her name remains exactly the same. Her children, however, take their father's name.

Arab names sometimes also indicate tribal affiliation and the village or region of origin. For example a man named Abd al Rahman ibn Qasim ibn Mohammed El Bayadh would be recognized as the son of Qasim, the grandson of Mohammed, and a native of the town of El Bayadh. The man would be addressed as Mister (or his title, if any) Abd al Rahman; in spoken Arabic, names are elided, so that in this instance the name would be pronounced as if it were spelled *Abdur Rahman*. In many instances the Western press spells such names as *Abdel* (or *Abdul*) *Rahman*, implying incorrectly that the man's first name is Abdel and his last name Rahman. Many Arabic names, such as the one in this example, are designations of the attributes of God (Allah). *Abd al* means "servant of," and *Rahman* means "merciful"; thus the name literally means "the servant of the Merciful (God)."

ARTS

AFTER INDEPENDENCE FROM FRENCH RULE, the government placed great emphasis on restoring Algeria's national, especially Arab, heritage. Each administration called for a revival of the art forms that had disappeared during the colonial period. Funds were allocated to restore historic monuments and archaeological sites and to create libraries and museums that recounted Algerian history.

The government also opened handicraft centers around the country to encourage the ancient crafts of rug making, pottery, embroidery, jewelry making, and brass work. Today Algeria has a thriving handicrafts industry. The center of traditional Algerian carpet making is in Ghardaia in the northern Sahara. Carpet patterns vary from region to region, but the best-known pattern is the *Souf* (SOO-oof), a broad cross set against a subtly shaded background. Tuareg sabers are also prized by art aficionados for their elegant shape, intricate hand-engraved decorations, and camel-skin sheaths. The National Institute of Music, meanwhile, has reintroduced traditional music, dance, and folklore originating from ancient Arabia and Moorish Spain.

Throughout the struggle for independence and during the civil war many Algerian artists, including moviemakers, writers, and actors, were killed for being politically outspoken. As a result many Algerian artists left the country to work abroad, mainly in France. Increasingly, as is true elsewhere in the world, Algeria is experiencing a clash between traditional and mass global culture, with Hollywood films and Western popular music fast gaining favor with the young at the expense of traditional forms of artistic and cultural expression.

Above: **A man carefully places pottery in storage. Pottery is a common handicraft in Algeria.**

Opposite: **A woman weaving at a loom. Algeria is famous for its rug making and embroidery.**

RAI

Rai (RYE) began as tribal music in the countryside around Oran, a seacoast city with notoriously uninhibited traditions that has been a meeting place for various musical traditions, including Arab, French, Spanish, and African. *Rai* in Arabic literally means "opinion." In Oran it is widely said that in the past, people often went to a learned man to ask for his opinion expressed in the form of poetry. The word *rai* also appears in the expression *ba-rai*, a sort of ancestor of the modern "oh yeah." This was the music's omnipresent refrain, so the music became known as *rai*. An important element of *rai* is that it is danceable, with simple but characteristic lyrics. Although rosewood flutes and rudimentary tambourines still accompany *rai*, it has also incorporated Western instruments such as drum machines and synthesizers into its repertoire, creating a kind of urban music.

In the beginning, *rai* was performed mainly at traditional festivals and weddings. Due to urbanization in the early 20th century some people from Relizane (east of Oran) migrated to Oran, where they performed at weddings, parties, bars, and lounges.

The music then began to evolve into what is now recognizable as *rai*—a blend of Berber, Moroccan, Spanish, and French music. The format of *rai* comes from *meddahas* (MAD-DAH-huss)—female poets and singers who sang Arabic love poetry. The female singers of the 1920s and 1930s sang in deep voices and were accompanied by rosewood flutes and various percussion instruments.

In the 1950s a lot of horn instruments were added, as well as the accordion and some violin—and modern *rai* was born. Big names of the 1950s and 1960s were Cheikh Boualem, Belabbas, Hourari, and Bellemou Messaoud. This modern *rai* was influenced by jazz and cha-cha.

RAI MUSICIANS UNDER ATTACK

During the civil war, *rai* music was accused of spreading corrupt Western values among the young (who in Algeria represented a good 75 percent of the population). Thus, more or less all *rai* stars are condemned to death by Islamic fundamentalists. Some militant religious leaders called for a fatwa, an order to all Muslims to kill a particular person, on singers they disliked. "What the terrorists want to show," said Cheb Khaled, the recognized king of *rai*, "is that you can continue to sing *rai* only abroad or in hiding. ... You can expect only the worst from people who fight to spread their own unhappiness to everyone." Cheb Khaled has since lived in self-imposed exile in Paris. *Rai* musicians continue to be controversial, lacing their lyrics with social and political criticism. (*Pictured here, a musician plays the* ghita, *a traditional musical instrument of Algeria.*)

By the late 1970s some producers started "pop *rai*," which uses synthesizers to duplicate the original sounds. Pop *rai* vocalized the powerlessness young people felt and, less explicitly, the discontent regarding political inertia and social inflexibility in Algeria. Modern *rai* emphasizes strong pleasures and the inevitable pains of existence: the joy of sex, the pain of love, food, alcohol, unemployment, and the daily grind.

Besides having made *rai* the other Algerian export besides oil, new stars such as Cheb Khaled rapidly transformed their music into a vehicle of youthful rebellion. That has put them on a collision course with Islamic extremism. The austere Islamic-socialist state condemned *rai* for its lascivious rhythms and often licentious lyrics but allowed it to function underground as a sort of pressure-release valve.

Until the 1980s little or nothing was known of *rai* outside Algeria, partly because the music was mostly on cassette tapes of anything but professional standards. *Rai* crossed over to France in the mid-1980s and then went global. In 1986 the first state-sanctioned *rai* festival was held in Algeria. In the late 1990s funk, hip-hop, and other influences were added to *rai*. Popular *rai* singers in Algeria include Cheb Mami, Sawt el Atlas, Cheb Tarik, Chaba Fadela, and Cheb Sahraoui.

Wahrani *(the music of Oran), blends* rai *with classical Algerian music of the Arab-Andalusian tradition.*

LITERATURE

When Algeria was under French rule many Algerian-born French writers flourished in the country. The most famous of these writers was Albert Camus.

From 1920, when the first Algerian novel was published (*Ahmed Ben Mostapha, goumier* by Ben Chérif), until 1950, Algerian literature tended to copy French models.

In the early 1950s a change took place in the literature, which began an interrogation on Algerian identity and the place of the writer in Algeria. Writers such as Mouloud Feraoun, Mohammed Dib, Mouloud Mammeri, and Malek Ouary began to proclaim their difference from French culture.

The war of independence produced a literature of combat, evident in the work of Dib, Mammeri, Kateb Yacine, and Malek Haddad. Haddad's *Le Malheur en danger* (*Distress in Danger*) started an interest in poetry. Assia Djebar became known for her novels highlighting the situation of women. Journals were also an important part of linguistic production during this period, especially those of Djamal Amrani, Mouloud Feraoun, and Ahmed Taleb Ibrahimi. Interestingly, many Algerian writers used French as their language instead of Arabic.

After the war of independence another period began, characterized by a questioning of earlier themes. Dib's work became quite personal and modernist. Yacine produced plays in Arabic. Nabile Farès pleaded for pluralism and openness, followed by Ali Bouhmadi and Mouloud Achour. The poetry of Noureddine Aba, Hamid Tibouchi, Tahar Djaout, and Malek Alloula is of particular interest.

Although most of Algeria's writers continue to live in exile in France and other parts of Europe, the literary scene is kept alive today by the Paris-based association Algérie Littérature/Action. Since 1996 the association has made significant contributions publishing contemporary Algerian fiction. Its founders are trying to revitalize the literary scene in Algeria. Contemporary Algerian writers include Aziz Chaouki, Ahlam Mosteghanemi, and poets Samia Dahnaan and Nafissa Boudalia.

ALBERT CAMUS

Albert Camus, born in Mondovi (modern Drean), Algeria, on November 7, 1913, earned a worldwide reputation as a novelist and essayist and won the Nobel Prize for literature in 1957. Born in extreme poverty, Camus attended lycée and university in Algiers, where he developed an abiding interest in sports and the theater. In 1937 he became a journalist with *Alger-Republicain*, an anticolonialist newspaper. While working for this daily he wrote detailed reports on the condition of poor Arabs in the Kabylia region.

During World War II Camus published the main works associated with his doctrine of the absurd—his view that human life is rendered ultimately meaningless by the fact of death and that the individual cannot make rational sense of his experience. These works include the novel *The Stranger* (1942), perhaps his finest work of fiction, and *The Myth of Sisyphus* (1942).

From this point on, Camus was concerned mainly with exploring avenues of rebellion against the absurd as he strove to create something like humane stoicism. *The Plague* (1947) is a symbolic novel in which the important achievement of those who fight bubonic plague in Oran lies not in the little success they have but in their assertion of human dignity

Through his writings, and in some measure against his will, Camus became the leading moral voice of his generation during the 1950s.

and endurance. In the controversial essay "The Rebel" (1951), he argued in favor of Mediterranean humanism, advocating nature and moderation rather than historicism and violence. Camus died in an automobile accident near Sens, France, in 1960, at the height of his fame.

LITERATURE'S LOSSES

Many writers have died directly or indirectly during the civil war because of their criticism of FIS militants. The poet Youcef Sebti was one casualty of this literary hit list. Another was Rachid Mimouni, who died in January 1995 of hepatitis contracted in Morocco, where he lived following threats by fundamentalists in Algeria. Mimouni's novel *The Curse*, winner of the Prix du Levant, focuses on political events in Algeria during the few years prior to its publication in 1993. Women, a chief concern of FIS militants, are at the center of his novel. As one of his characters says, "They need an enemy, a great Satan who can crystallize the causes of all evil. And, well, the Jews have served that purpose already." His women characters drink, smoke, swear; by contrast, the only veiled woman in the novel, an FIS militant, is ridiculed, as is Algeria's military government.

Another casualty was novelist Tahar Djaout, killed in 1993. Djaout was considered to be the heir of the writers of the so-called 1952 Generation who included Mohammed Dib, Mouloud Mammeri, Mouloud Feraoun, and Kateb Yacine. A native of Azzefoun, Kabylia, Djaout moved to Algiers to complete his education. In 1974 he became a journalist, first with *El Moujahid* and then with *Algérie-Actualité*. In 1993 he founded the weekly *Ruptures* with friends and was its chief editor until his death. Influenced by the ethnological writings of Feraoun and the poetic writings of Yacine, Djaout explored the past and the present, incorporating the history of North Africa, the colonization of Algeria, and his childhood experience in Kabylia. His last three novels described aspects of a search for an identity illustrated by the narrators' journeys in space and time.

Djaout strongly disapproved of the government's control of public life. In *Les Chercheurs d'os* (*Searchers for Bones*), set in the aftermath of the war of independence, the plot revolves around the retrieval of the remains of Algerian combatants for reburial. The quest for his older brother's remains requires a young villager to undertake his first journey outside his home. Upon his return with his brother's remains, the young man questions the purpose of the quest for bones, suggesting that the villagers, in fact, fear the combatants' ghosts and that an official and deeper burial of the bones would offer more reassurance. He realizes that the villagers are deader than the combatants whose remains are being reburied.

Tahar Djaout, killed at the age of 39, was another great loss to Algerian literature.

Les Vigiles (*The Vigils*) reflects on the corrosive nature of Algerian society during the reign of the FLN government. The story is about a young Algerian teacher who has developed an innovative and efficient weaving loom. He wishes to register and patent his invention but is hampered by a number of inextricable bureaucratic difficulties.

Djaout's death inspired a surge of artistic production often referred to as the *littérature d'urgence*, or "literature of urgency." He soon became the symbol for resistance against intimidation and violence in Algeria. The tremendous spurt of literary expression during the civil war deals with the conflict and its effects on the people. This type of politically engaged writing continues to be seen today and is characteristic of Algerian literature since before independence.

CINEMA

The Algerian art form that has earned the greatest acclaim in Algeria and worldwide is the cinema. Most Algerian movies are produced by the national film company, ONAPROC. Algerians have won several international film festival awards for dramas and documentaries about colonialism, revolution, and controversial social topics. Mohamed Lakhdar Hamina won a 1975 Cannes Film Festival award for *Chronique des années de braise* (*Chronicle of the Years of Fire*), which was about the Algerian fight for independence from a peasant's viewpoint. Hamina was also nominated for a Palme d'Or award at the 1982 Cannes Film Festival for *Desert Wind*, which showcased the difficult lives Algerian women confront in a traditional society.

Director Belkacem Hadjaj's *The Drop* (1982/1989) presents the plight of rural migrants with dark melancholia. Slogging on housing in which they cannot afford to live, the migrant workers are portrayed as victims of blatant and appalling exploitation by the city. Cold grinding tractor gears and endless hammering serving as an allusion to their toils and pain, even their sweat is symbolically and grimly collected in an urn.

Mohamed Rachid Benhadj's *Desert Rose* (1989) relates the intimate story of Mousa, a severely handicapped young man. Told matter-of-factly, it tells of the protagonist's will to overcome his infirmities as he searches for love and society's recognition in a remote oasis village.

Merzak Allouache's *Bab El-Oued City* (1994), set in early 1993, depicts the dangers inherent in the recent rise of Islamic fundamentalism in Algeria. Bab El-Oued is a working-class district of Algiers. One morning shortly after the bloody riots of October 1988, Boualem, a young employee in a bakery who works at night and sleeps during the day, commits an act that puts the entire district in turmoil: Unable to stand the noise from

THE DEVIL IN THE FEMININE CASE

Director Hafsa Zinai Koudil, a tense, chain-smoking woman, got her idea for a movie from a true story reported in 1990. A man had his wife beaten up by exorcists because she refused to wear the veil. Her attackers were brought to justice but given only token sentences.

The Devil in the Feminine Case describes an urban couple whose eldest son is won over to the cause of Islamic fundamentalism. His father also espouses the cause. The two become obsessed with the idea of getting the mother to wear the veil. When she refuses, they declare that she is possessed by the devil and hire three men to exorcise her. The torture session ends with the woman rushed to the hospital. She is handicapped for life, and her husband goes out of his mind.

"I made the film in an atmosphere of terror," said Koudil. She had no police protection, and throughout the filming crew members took turns to look out for signs of trouble. The film was not distributed in Algeria. *The Devil in the Feminine Case* was shown, however, at the 1994 Amiens Festival and at the 1995 International Women's Film Festival.

Koudil is also the author of four novels, the first being the autobiographical *The End of a Dream* in 1984. Her most recent novel, *The Discomposed Past*, published in 1992, denounces the status of women in Algeria.

one of the many rooftop loudspeakers broadcasting the propaganda of a fundamentalist group, he rips out the speaker and throws it away. The extremists, led by Said, regard the removal of the speaker as provocative and want to make an example of him. Violence escalates when Said's younger sister is caught meeting Boualem, with whom she is secretly in love.

Bab El-Oued City attracted considerable attention, winning both an International Film Critics prize and a Prix Gervais at the 1994 Cannes Film Festival. During the shooting of *Bab El-Oued City*, violence fully erupted in Algeria. Allouache shot some of the exterior scenes with a camera hidden under his coat.

Since 1995 only one or two Algerian films have been produced a year. The lack of funds coupled with the shutting down of movie theaters across the country has stymied the production of films. It was therefore timely that the Ministry of Culture recently decided to lay the foundations for a new filmmaking institution, the Centre National de la Cinématographie et de l'Audiovisuel (CNCA), with funding assured. Many filmmakers take this as a sign of the reawakening of Algerian filmmaking. Recent Algerian productions include *Barakat!*, *Bab el Web*, and *Alienations*.

LEISURE

ALGERIAN SOCIAL LIFE revolves around visiting family. The family is not only the most important unit of the Algerian social system, but it also defines social relations. Relatives call on each other frequently to share sweet treats and lengthy conversation. Outsiders are rarely invited, but when they are, they are treated with great hospitality and generosity. Hospitality is an important characteristic for all Arabs as well as Berbers. A traditional Berber saying expresses the Algerian emphasis on hospitality: "When you come to our house, it is we who are your guests, for this is your home."

Similar to other Mediterranean peoples, Algerians like to go to beaches. The Algerian middle class enjoys summer resorts along the coast. Popular resorts include Zeralda in Algiers and Les Andalouses in Oran. Here families swim, water-ski, play tennis, and fish at modern facilities. Most families vacation in August, which is when most Algerians who work in Europe return home.

Algerians play basketball, volleyball, and handball, but soccer by far is the most popular sport. In 1982 and 1986 Algeria qualified for the World Cup, and it even won the Africa Nations Cup in 1990. People of all ages play and watch soccer matches. Young boys can be seen kicking balls outside city housing projects. However, in rural areas, boys must tend their sheep rather than play. Girls are less visible at play. They are expected to help their mothers.

Children in Algeria love to play dominoes and a game similar to hopscotch. A snake shape is drawn on the ground, with boxes numbered

Above: **Men converse in a park. Women spend less time in public.**

Opposite: **Going to the beach is fast becoming a popular pastime among Algerians.**

Men spend many leisure hours at outdoor cafés.

from 1 to 20, including five "jail" boxes. The players pit themselves against each other, one on one, or two against two, and so on. They take turns throwing bottle tops into the boxes. If a bottle top lands on a "jail" box, the owner has to start all over again from the first box. The first player to reach the box numbered 20 is the winner.

As children get older, girls are seen even less, and boys take to city streets. Young men, especially the unemployed, hang around street corners and cafés looking for activity. Despite the size of some cities, there is very little to do outside of home, school, and work.

LEISURELY PURSUITS

Life moves at a leisurely pace in Algeria. Algerians do not rush around frantically trying to do a million things. Most leisure activities in Algeria are family oriented.

116

A DIFFICULT TIME FOR WOMEN IN SPORTS

In 1991 Hassiba Boulmerka became the first African woman to win a gold medal at the World Track and Field Championships when she won the 1,500-meter run. A year later in Barcelona she became Algeria's first Olympic champion, winning the 1,500-meter run in 3 minutes 55.3 seconds.

Whether her achievements instill pride or fury in her countrymen depends, she said, on whom one asks. "In general, I get positive reactions in Algeria because I'm a symbol of my country. But like every symbol, there are some who like me and some who don't." Every time she runs in shorts, she incurs the wrath of Muslim fundamentalists, who have spat on her, pelted her with rocks, and called her blasphemous for "running with naked legs in front of thousands of men."

Although she lives abroad nine months out of the year, she returns to Algeria regularly to try to be a role model for girls there. Some school sports programs similar to the one that spawned her career have been discontinued. "The situation is difficult in Algeria, especially for women," Boulmerka said. "But it's important to have courage and set an example by training there, so I do. It'll never be easy for women in Algeria. But my gold medal wasn't simply a victory for the moment. It was a victory for the future. It gave a glimpse of what women could do in Algeria."

Another Algerian woman to excel in track and field is Nouria Merah-Benida. She won the gold medal at the 2000 Summer Olympics in Sydney for her 1,500-meter run. That same year she won the silver medal for the 800-meter race and the gold for the 1,500-meter race at the African Championships. In 1999 at the All-Africa Games in Johannesburg she won the silver in both the 800-meter and the 1,500-meter events.

Although its promotion of women in sports is far from ideal, Algeria has taken small steps in encouraging women's participation. The government has established the National Association for the Promotion and Development of Women's Sports and a women's football club, CabashFC, based in Algiers. For the first time in Algerian history a Women's National Championship for Football was played in front of 80,000 fans in 1999.

Algerians enjoy eating well but do not eat out often. Most Algerians savor eating good traditional food at home in the company of friends and extended family. They welcome any excuse for a banquet. Women, who tend to socialize almost exclusively at home, especially enjoy these get-togethers.

Men are less restricted in their movement and tend to congregate in cafés to play dominoes or chess or to discuss local affairs and events and to exchange gossip over coffee, mint tea, or a refreshing *sharbat* (SHAAR-but), which is a fruit- or nut-flavored milk drink poured over shaved ice.

FESTIVALS

ALGERIA'S MAJOR RELIGIOUS holidays, including Eid al-Fitr, Eid al-Adha, Muharram, and Mawlid an-Nabi, have long histories going back to the founding of Islam. They fall on different dates of the Western calendar each year because they are linked to the Muslim calendar rather than the Gregorian calendar. The Gregorian calendar is solar, while the Muslim calendar is lunar; therefore the Muslim year is 11 days shorter than the Gregorian year.

Above: **The opening ceremony of the Horse Festival in Tiaret.**

Opposite: **Algerian Djanet women playing drums in celebration of the Sebiba Festival in the Sahara Desert.**

EID AL-ADHA

Also called Eid al-Kebir, or the Major Festival, Eid al-Adha is celebrated on the 10th of Dhu al-Hijja, the last month of the lunar year. Although Muslims observe this holiday in their hometowns all around the world, its most sacred observance is in Mina, a small village four miles (6.4 km) east of Mecca. There hundreds of thousands of Muslims observe the animal sacrifice as part of the hajj, the pilgrimage to Mecca and other sacred sites nearby.

The teachings of Muhammad decree that heads of families who are able to do so must purchase a sheep for sacrifice. The meat of the slaughtered animal is shared with the poor; the Prophet recommended giving one-third to the poor, one-third to neighbors and friends, and letting one-third remain in the family. The sacrifice signifies the willingness of Ibrahim (known to Christians and Jews as Abraham) to sacrifice what was most precious to him, his son. As Ibrahim prepared to kill his son, God stopped him and gave him a sheep to sacrifice instead. The sacrificer symbolically affirms that he is willing to give up, for the sake of God, that which is dearest to him. It is a sacred gesture of thanksgiving and a measure of charity.

Festival celebrants in southern Algeria.

Like Eid al-Fitr, Eid al-Adha is traditionally a family gathering. For pilgrims camped at Mina, it also marks the end of their pilgrimage and a return to normal life.

EID AL-FITR

Also called Eid al-Sagheer, or the Minor Festival, this holiday occurs on the first day of the month of Shawwal, immediately after Ramadan, the fasting month. Eid al-Fitr begins with the men going to the mosque for the morning prayer. This is followed, according to the teachings of the Prophet, by a visit to the cemetery.

These solemn religious expressions then change into a happy festival in the homes of heads of families. Gifts and money are given to children and to newly married daughters. More significant is the joyous return for all to a normal life. Islamic law requires that *zakat al-fitr* (ZAAR-kaht-el-fee-tree), or the alms of breaking the fast, be given to the poor.

This festival brings Algeria to a standstill for at least two days, although feasting and festivities often continue for up to a week. People in Algeria prepare by scrubbing their houses and painting the shutters. Special food is prepared well in advance, and new clothes are bought for the occasion. On the holiday, everyone dresses up in his or her best clothes and brings pastries to friends and relatives.

MAWLID AN-NABI

Prophet Muhammad's birthday is celebrated on the 12th day of the third Islamic month, Rebbi ul-awal. This festival was not observed by the Muslim faithful until the 13th century. For one thing, the exact date of Prophet Muhammad's birth was not known. By the ninth century a set body of traditions about the teachings of the Prophet had become standardized. One precedent in Muhammad's life that emerged was that many important events had occurred on Mondays. His *hegira*, or journey, to Medina and his death were thought by many to have occurred on

Mondays. Tradition formed in favor of Monday, the 12th day of Rebbi ul-awal, as the anniversary of his birth.

Mawlid an-Nabi has become a major religious festival for Muslims in the Islamic world, and Algeria is no exception. This day is observed with special prayers. Men congregate at the local mosque or make a special journey to the main mosque to hear the imam tell the story of Prophet Muhammad's life. Women gather in each other's homes for prayers.

HORSE AND CAMEL FESTIVALS

In the desert regions, traditional horse and camel festivals are celebrated. Two of the better-known festivals are the Horse Festival of Tiaret and

PUBLIC HOLIDAYS

New Year's Day: January 1
Labor Day: May 1
Commemoration Day (anniversary of the overthrow of Mohamed Ahmed Ben Bella in a bloodless coup d'état): June 19
Independence Day: July 5
Anniversary of the Revolution (commemorates the first well-coordinated attack by the National Liberation Front against the French): November 1
Eid al-Fitr: variable
Eid al-Adha: variable
Mawlid an-Nabi (Prophet Muhammad's birthday): variable

OTHER HOLIDAYS

Leilat al-Meiraj (ascension of Prophet Muhammad): variable
Al-Hijra (Islamic New Year's Day): variable
Ashoura: variable

the Camel Festival celebrated in Metlili, near Ghardaia. During the Horse Festival, there are horse races and parades, with riders from other regions represented. There is also a competition called Fantasia, in which the riders must aim and shoot at a target while their horses are in full gallop and then bring their horses to an abrupt stop.

The Camel Festival at Metlili lasts two full days in March. There is a Fantasia at this one too. Another popular event is camel dancing, where the camel riders make their camels dance to the accompaniment of traditional instruments. For a percussion effect, the riders shoot their rifles into the ground, which makes the ground vibrate under the spectators' feet. There is also a bride parade, a traditional custom that goes back to ancient times.

A camel race draws a large crowd of spectators. Families from the surrounding areas come by the truckload or in caravans to attend.

FOOD

TRADITIONAL ALGERIAN CUISINE is rich in variety and delights the senses with special seasonings. Coriander is the chief flavoring throughout the Maghrib region. In Algeria chefs also include ginger, hot peppers, pimiento, cumin, caraway, marjoram, mint, cinnamon, onions, garlic, cloves, and parsley in their dishes.

The agricultural areas of Algeria specialize in lemons, olives, tomatoes, peppers, dates, grapes, potatoes, almonds, and figs. Fish and other seafood are available along the coast. Nomadic peoples rear chickens, sheep, goats, cattle, and horses. No pork is served, due to religious beliefs.

Algerian cuisine and cooking methods reflect the mix of cultures. The Berbers traditionally cooked stews of lamb, poultry, and vegetables. The Arabs introduced spices and mouthwatering pastries. The French chiefly contributed their use of tomato purees and incomparable breads, and some Spanish influence can be seen in the use of olives and olive oil.

COUSCOUS

Couscous is often, but incorrectly, described as a grain. It is actually a type of pasta made from dough that contains durum wheat (semolina) and water. Instead of being rolled out or extruded to form noodles, the dough is rubbed through a sieve to make tiny pellets. The word *couscous* is derived from the Arabic *kuskusu*, which means "to pound well," though some cooking experts believe couscous is onomatopoeic for the sound of the pellets hitting the water.

But couscous also refers to a style of eating in North Africa, where stews are made with couscous. The couscous arrives in a steaming mound on a platter. A spicy stew is ladled over the couscous, followed by a spoonful of *harissa* (HAAR-ree-sar), a fiery condiment made with hot pimientos. Often, for extra flavor, the couscous is steamed over the

Opposite: **A wide variety of herbs and spices can be found at the Tamanrasset market.**

SERVING AND EATING ALGERIAN COUSCOUS

1.   Make a salad of sliced ripe tomatoes topped with morsels of oil-packed canned tuna, chopped onion, and anchovies; drizzle with olive oil and generously splash on lemon juice. Set it in the middle of a large platter, and spoon the couscous around it.

2.   Make a salad of peeled sliced oranges, thinly sliced radishes, and finely chopped mint leaves. Sprinkle with a dressing of orange juice sharpened by a dash of vinegar. Serve on the same platter as the couscous.

3.   For dessert, pour the warm couscous in the center of a platter, and sprinkle with chopped sticky dates, shelled almonds, and chopped fresh or dried figs. Eat dessert couscous by dipping the right-hand fingers into the mixture and making a small ball, then eating it off your fingers.

stew. Like pasta, couscous can accommodate an almost endless variety of toppings and sauces.

Couscous is a staple throughout North Africa and is believed to have been eaten since Roman times. Moroccan couscous is the mildest, lightest, and fluffiest, while Algerian couscous is firm and dense. Couscous also turns up in Sicily, where it is served with seafood, and in Tunisia, where one version calls for pomegranates and orange-flower water and is served as a dessert.

Couscous is probably Algeria's most popular dish and is often called its national dish. The Mediterranean and Middle Eastern countries each have their own preferences and recipes for making couscous. In Algeria stews are simmered slowly for several hours until everything in the pot is blended together and the meat falls off the bones. Couscous is usually served surrounded by lamb or chicken in a bed of cooked vegetables and covered with gravy. Often onions, turnips, raisins, garbanzo beans, and red bell peppers are added. *Harissa* is always served with Algerian couscous and is enjoyed by those who are accustomed to hot foods. Couscous mixed with honey, cinnamon, and almonds makes a dessert that tastes similar to rice pudding.

BREAD

Bread is a staple of the Algerian diet. For many poor people, bread teamed with a few olives or dates, or perhaps a small piece of goat cheese, is a meal in itself. This is usually accompanied by a glass of hot mint tea.

Bread, usually French loaf, is eaten at every meal. In addition to being an accompaniment to whatever other food is being served, crusty chunks are useful for scooping up meat and vegetables and for soaking up the spicy gravy that usually flavors Algerian stews. Berbers eat traditional flat cakes of mixed grains, while bread is also a traditional part of the Arab diet.

Wheat is the basis of the Algerian diet, whether it is in the form of bread or couscous. Many sayings highlight the importance of bread in traditional Algerian society.

LAMB

Lamb is one of the mainstays of Algerian cuisine. It is eaten grilled, minced for use as a vegetable stuffing, or used as a main ingredient in stews and couscous.

A favorite lamb dish is *mechoui* (meshwee), which is charcoal-roasted whole lamb. *Mechoui* is a favorite dish for large gatherings and picnics. A Berber specialty, *mechoui* is prepared by rubbing the lamb with garlic and spices. The lamb is then roasted over an open-air spit at the beach

Roasting a whole lamb on a spit in Timimoun.

or in the village or the garden. It is basted regularly with herbed butter so that it becomes crispy on the outside and soft and tender on the inside. The best *mechoui* is so tender that the crisp skin peels away easily and the meat comes away in the hand. Guests pluck bits of lamb from the roast to eat with bread, usually French bread. Other accompaniments to *mechoui* include various dried fruits, such as dates, and vegetables.

MEDITERRANEAN SPECIALTIES

Algeria shares most of its culinary mainstays with the other countries of the Mediterranean region. Dishes such as tabbouleh and hummus are found throughout the Mediterranean, especially in the Middle East, although the spicing may vary somewhat. For instance, Middle Eastern tabbouleh uses more lemon and less oil than that prepared in Algeria. Chickpeas, sesame paste, olives, dates, and lemons are common ingredients in Algerian cooking. Desserts such as baklava, usually associated with Greek cooking, are also found in Algeria. Mint tea is a favorite throughout the region.

DRINKS

The most popular drink in North Africa is mint-flavored tea, and Algeria is no exception. However, other drinks abound, and fruit-drink stands are plentiful, piled high with fruits in season and tempting glasses of juice on display. Orange juice, sugarcane juice, and lemon juice are popular. Drinks made from other citrus fruits, pomegranates, and grapes are also favorites. Children are usually offered a glass of sweet apricot juice.

FIGS

Figs comprise a large genus, *Ficus*, of deciduous and evergreen tropical and subtropical trees, shrubs, and vines belonging to the mulberry family. Commercially the most important fig is *Ficus carica*, the tree that produces the edible fig fruit. Among the most ancient cultivated fruit trees, the fig is indigenous to the eastern Mediterranean and the southwest region of Asia, where its cultivation probably began. It is now grown in warm, semiarid areas throughout the world.

The fruit-bearing fig ranges from a bushlike 3 feet (1 m) to a moderately tall tree that may grow up to 39 feet (12 m) in height. It is characterized by dark green, deeply lobed leaves.

The fig bears no visible flowers; its flowers are borne within a round, fleshy structure, the syconium, which matures into the edible fig. The common fig bears only female flowers but develops its fruits without pollination. Varieties of the Smyrna type also bear only female flowers, but to produce fruit they must be pollinated artificially.

Fig trees are propagated through rooted cuttings taken from the wood of older trees. They grow best in moderately dry areas that have no rain during the period of fruit maturation; during this period humidity might hinder the process of fruit drying, much of which occurs on the tree. The partially dried fruit drops to the ground, where it is gathered and the drying process completed. Some fruit may be picked from the tree before it dries and eaten as fresh fruit.

Also popular are *sharbats*, which are milk drinks that are fruit- or nut-flavored. Refreshing yogurt-based drinks flavored with fruit or nuts are also found at these drink stands.

Algerians are also fond of coffee and drink it in various forms. Thick black coffee is most common, but coffee is also served half and half—half coffee and half hot milk. Spices such as cloves, cinnamon, and cardamom are also added to coffee. *Ras el hanout* , an ancient coffee drink originally from Morocco, is mixed with anywhere from 10 to 26 spices.

Berbers prefer drinks made from goat's milk. A traditional Berber drink is made from goat cheese. The cheese is crumbled and crushed with dates and well water. This drink is almost a complete meal in itself and is most often drunk by nomadic goat herders.

CHORBA BIL MATISHA (SOUP WITH CAPELLINI AND VEGETABLES)

This recipe serves four.

1 large onion
4 whole cloves
6 cups vegetable broth
2 pounds butternut squash, cubed
4 stalks celery, chopped
2 cans diced tomatoes

2 tablespoons cilantro, finely chopped
$1/4$ teaspoon turmeric
$1/4$ cup capellini or angel-hair pasta, broken
1 cup milk
Salt and pepper, according to taste
1 large lemon, wedged

Holding the large onion steady, carefully stud it with the cloves. In a soup pot, combine the onion, broth, squash, celery, tomatoes, cilantro, and turmeric. Over a high heat, bring the soup to a boil. Then reduce the heat to medium, and cook for another 30 minutes or until the vegetables are tender. Once the vegetables are ready, discard the onion and cloves. Pour the soup into a blender and puree until smooth.

Return the soup to the pot and add the pasta. Simmer for another eight minutes. Later, add milk to thin the soup. Once the milk is warmed through, season the soup with salt and pepper. Ladle the soup onto a serving bowl and serve with lemon wedges.

ALGERIAN CHARLOTTE

This recipe serves six to eight.

Juice of 1 orange	$\frac{1}{2}$ cup chopped almonds
1 $\frac{1}{2}$ cups water	2 cups heavy cream
3 tablespoons honey	2 tablespoons sliced almonds
1 tablespoon gelatin	2 chopped dates
1 cup dates, pitted and quartered	Grated peel of $\frac{1}{2}$ orange

In a saucepan, over a medium flame, pour the juice of an orange. Add water and honey. Stir in the gelatin. Once it is dissolved, add in the quartered dates. When the mixture comes to a boil, reduce heat, cover saucepan, and simmer for 30 minutes. Then switch off the flame and let mixture cool. Strain the mixture, reserving the liquid in a bowl. Add the chopped almonds to reserved liquid.

Next, whip the cream in another bowl until it forms peaks. Gently fold the liquid into the cream. Chill the charlotte in the refrigerator for two or more hours before serving. To serve, spoon the charlotte into a serving dish (or dessert glasses) and decorate it with sliced almonds, chopped dates, and grated orange peel.

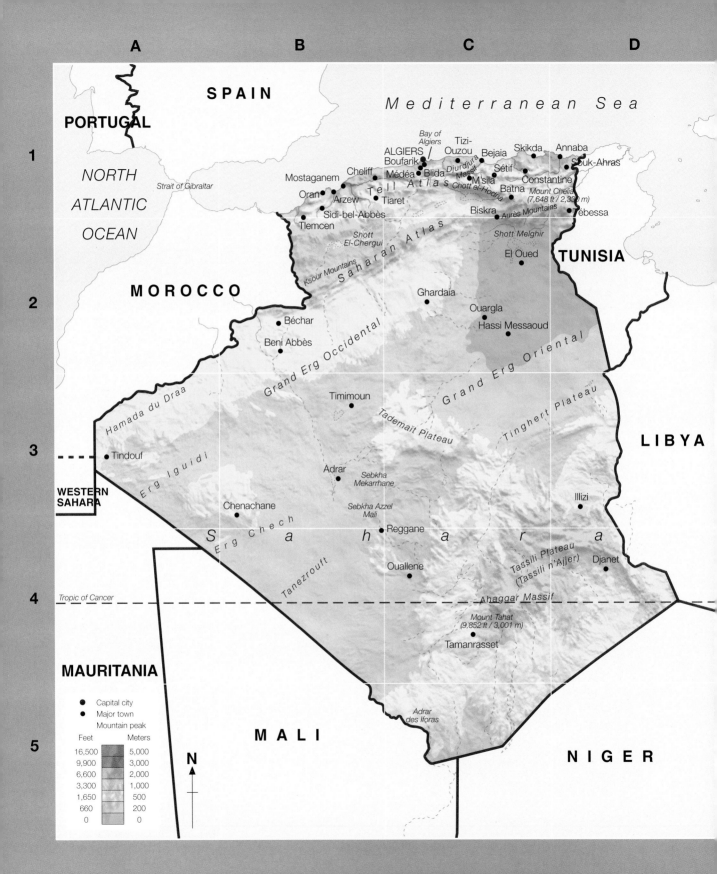

A **B** **C** **D**

1
2
3
4
5

SPAIN

PORTUGAL

Mediterranean Sea

NORTH

ATLANTIC

OCEAN

Strait of Gibraltar

Bay of Algiers

Tizi-Ouzou
ALGIERS
Boufarik
Mostaganem
Cheliff
Médéa
Blida
Djurdjura
Bejaia
Skikda
Annaba
Souk-Ahras
Massif
Sétif
Constantine
Oran
Arzew
Tiaret
M'sila
Batna
Chott el-Hodna
Mount Chelia
(7,648 ft / 2,330 m)
Sidi-bel-Abbès
Biskra
Tébessa
Tlemcen
Aurès Mountains

Tell Atlas

MOROCCO

Shott El-Chergui
Shott Melghir

El Oued
TUNISIA

Ksour Mountains
Saharan Atlas

Ghardaia

Béchar

Ouargla

Beni Abbès
Hassi Messaoud

Grand Erg Occidental
Grand Erg Oriental

Hamada du Draa

Timimoun
Tademaït Plateau
Tinghert Plateau

LIBYA

Erg Iguidi

Tindouf

Adrar
Sebkha Mekarrhane

Illizi

Chenachane
Sebkha Azzel Mali

WESTERN
SAHARA

S *a* *h* *a* *r* *a*
Reggane
Erg Chech

Tanezrouft
Ouallene
Tassili Plateau
(Tassili n'Ajjer)
Djanet

Tropic of Cancer
Ahaggar Massif

Mount Tahat
(9,852 ft / 3,001 m)

MAURITANIA
Tamanrasset

● Capital city
● Major town
▲ Mountain peak

Feet	Meters
16,500	5,000
9,900	3,000
6,600	2,000
3,300	1,000
1,650	500
660	200
0	0

N

MALI

Adrar des Iforas

NIGER

MAP OF ALGERIA

ECONOMIC ALGERIA

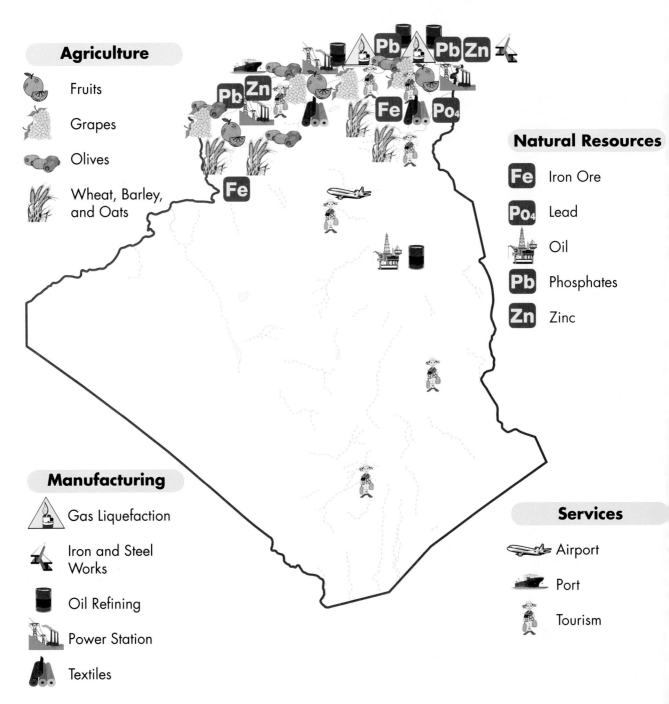

Agriculture

- Fruits
- Grapes
- Olives
- Wheat, Barley, and Oats

Natural Resources

- Fe Iron Ore
- Po₄ Lead
- Oil
- Pb Phosphates
- Zn Zinc

Manufacturing

- Gas Liquefaction
- Iron and Steel Works
- Oil Refining
- Power Station
- Textiles

Services

- Airport
- Port
- Tourism

ABOUT
THE ECONOMY

OVERVIEW

Algeria's economic development is largely focused on the marketing of its hydrocarbons industry. This state-controlled industry has vastly improved the country's economic outlook; currently its oil and gas exports account for more than 95 percent of its export earnings and 30 percent of its gross domestic product (GDP). This has allowed the country to significantly reduce its large foreign debt. Algeria is also diversifying its economy outside of the energy sector, which includes the development of its banking sector and the construction of infrastructure. However, a great number of the country's population is unemployed, and a quarter of its population is estimated to live below the poverty line.

GROSS DOMESTIC PRODUCT (GDP)

$250 billion (2006 estimate)

GDP GROWTH

3 percent (2006 estimate)

LAND USE

Arable land: 3.17 percent; permanent crops: 0.28 percent; other: 96.55 percent (2005 estimates)

CURRENCY

1 Algerian dinar (DZD) = 100 centimes
Notes: 1,000, 500, 200, 100, 50 DZD
Coins: 100, 50, 20, 10, 5, 2, 1 centimes
USD1 = 72.647 DZD (2006)

INFLATION RATE

3 percent (2006 estimate)

MINERAL RESOURCES

Petroleum, natural gas, iron ore, phosphates, uranium, lead, zinc

AGRICULTURAL PRODUCTS

Wheat, barley, oats, grapes, olives, citrus fruits, sheep, cattle

INDUSTRIES

Petroleum, natural gas, light industries, mining, electrical, petrochemical, food processing

MAJOR EXPORTS

Petroleum, natural gas, petroleum products

MAJOR IMPORTS

Capital goods, foodstuffs, consumer goods

TRADE PARTNERS

United States, Italy, Spain, France, Canada, Brazil, Belgium, Germany

EXTERNAL DEBT

$5 billion (2006 estimate)

WORKFORCE

9.31 million (2006 estimate)

UNEMPLOYMENT RATE

15.7 percent (2006 estimate)

AIRPORTS

142; 52 with paved runways, 90 without

CULTURAL ALGERIA

Casbah of Algiers
Among the capital's many landmarks, the labyrinthine Casbah of Algiers, built in Ottoman times, is the most iconic. This former fortress, surrounded by thick walls and maze-like alleys, still contains the remains of old mosques and Ottoman–style palaces.

Tipasa
The ruins of three churches—the Great Basilica, the Basilica Alexander and the Basilica of Saint Salsa—can be found at Tipasa, once one of the most important Christian settlements in North Africa. Tombs hewn out of solid rock can be found under the foundations of the Great Basilica.

M'Zab Valley
Five fortified cities dating back from the 10th century still stand well preserved in this 6.2-mile- (10-km-) long fertile valley, where more than 300,000 green date palms grow.

Tamanrasset
The navel of the Sahara, Tamanrasset is a small oasis town with a population of about 76,000. It is home to a large Tuareg population who are famed for their finely crafted swords, and camel and horse races. Tamanrasset's weather is actually mild as it is situated on hills that are elevated some 4,593.2 feet (1,400 m) above sea level. Camel rides are popular in this rocky and sandy desert.

Djemila Ruins
Djemila Ruins, situated 2,952.8 feet (900 m) above sea level, is considered to be one of North Africa's best-preserved Roman sites. Marble statues and a mosaic-decorated baptistery dating from the first century A.D. can still be seen. The Great Baths are also in almost perfect condition.

Timgad
Emperor Trajan constructed Timgad in A.D. 100 as a fortress against the Berbers. The ruins showed that Timgad was built according to a Roman town planning—a square enclosure with two perpendicular routes running through the city, complete with a forum in the center and a theater south of it.

Great Mosque of Al Qal'a
This World Heritage Site is noted for its ruins of a fortified Muslim city. It was one of the largest mosques in Algeria, with a large rectangular prayer room that held 13 aisles with eight bays. The 82-feet- (25-meter-) high minaret, one of the largest minarets of the Muslim world, is the only standing structure left today.

Tassili N'Ajjer
Tassili N'Ajjer was first established as a national park to protect its internationally important cultural heritage. A series of more than 15,000 ancient cave paintings, dating back to 6,000 B.C., records the climatic changes, animal migrations, and the evolution of human life on the edge of the Sahara.

ABOUT THE CULTURE

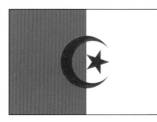

OFFICIAL NAME
Al Jumhuriyah al Jaza'iriyah ad Dimuqratiyah ash Sha'biyah (People's Democratic Republic of Algeria)

FLAG DESCRIPTION
Equal-size vertical bands of green (on hoist side) and white, with a red, five-pointed star within a red crescent in the center. The crescent, the star, and the color green are traditional symbols of Islam, which is Algeria's state religion.

TOTAL AREA
919,595 square miles (2,381,740 square km)

CAPITAL
Algiers

ETHNIC GROUPS
Arab–Berber 99 percent, European less than 1 percent

RELIGIOUS GROUPS
Sunni Muslim 99 percent, Christian and Jewish 1 percent

POPULATION
33.4 million (2007 estimate)

BIRTHRATE
17.11 births per 1,000 Algerians (2007 estimate)

DEATH RATE
4.62 deaths per 1,000 Algerians (2007 estimate)

AGE STRUCTURE
0–14 years: 27.2 percent (male 4,627,479/female 4,447,468);
15–64 years: 67.9 percent (male 11,413,121/female 11,235,096);
65 years and older: 4.8 percent (male 752,058/female 857,994) (2007 estimates)

LANGUAGES
Arabic (official national language), Tamazight (national language), French, Berber dialects

LITERACY RATE
Algerians of ages 15 and older who can read and write: 70 percent (2002 estimate)

NATIONAL HOLIDAYS
New Year's Day (January 1), Labor Day (May 1), Commemoration Day (June 19), Independence Day (July 5), Anniversary of the Revolution (November 1), Muharram/Islamic New Year (date varies), Ashoura (date varies), Eid al-Fitr (date varies), Eid al-Adha (date varies), Mawlid an–Nabi (date varies), Leilat al-Meiraj (date varies)

LEADERS IN POLITICS
Mohamed Ahmed Ben Bella—prime minister of Algeria (1962–63), president of Algeria (1963–65)
Houari Boumédienne—president of the Revolutionary Council (1965–76), president of Algeria (1976–78)
Abdelaziz Bouteflika—president of Algeria (1999–present)
Abdelaziz Belkhadem—prime minister of Algeria (2006–present)

TIME LINE

IN ALGERIA	IN THE WORLD
	753 B.C. Rome is founded.
500 B.C. Carthage, the greatest of the overseas Punic colonies, extends its hegemony across much of North Africa.	**116–17 B.C.** The Roman Empire reaches its greatest extent, under Emperor Trajan (98–17).
	A.D. 600 Height of the Mayan civilization
1200–1200 Decline of the Berber kingdoms. Arabs from Egypt and other areas of the Middle East begin settling into North Africa.	**1776** U.S. Declaration of Independence
1815 The United States declares war on Algiers to put an end to robberies by Barbary pirates.	**1789–99** The French Revolution
1830 French conquest of Algiers	
1837–1847 Algerian leader Abd al-Qadir is defeated in a revolt against France.	
1848 Central and western portion of Algeria is declared part of France.	**1869** The Suez Canal is opened.
1914–18 World War I. Thousands of Algerian Muslims help France during the war as soldiers or workers in defense plants in France.	**1914** World War I begins.
	1939 World War II begins.
1945 Algerians demonstrate for independence in Sétif and Constantine. The police open fire, killing thousands.	**1945** The United States drops atomic bombs on Hiroshima and Nagasaki.
1954–58 Algerian exiles in Egypt create the Front de Libération Nationale (FLN) and start the Algerian revolution.	**1949** The North Atlantic Treaty Organization (NATO) is formed.
1962 Algeria becomes independent on July 5.	

IN ALGERIA	IN THE WORLD
1963 After a power struggle within the FLN, Mohamed Ahmed Ben Bella becomes Algeria's first president.	
1965 Houari Boumédienne seizes power in a bloodless coup. He keeps Ben Bella under house arrest for 15 years.	**1966–69** The Chinese Cultural Revolution
1976 Boumédienne is elected president. He declares Algeria a socialist state and launches a program of rapid industrialization. Islam is recognized as state religion.	**1986** Nuclear power disaster at Chernobyl in Ukraine
1990 First multiparty elections since 1962 are won by the Front Islamique du Salut (FIS) by a large margin of votes.	**1991** Breakup of the Soviet Union
1992 Algerian army cancels national elections and seizes power. Mohamed Boudiaf takes over and chairs a five-member Higher State Council. A state of emergency is declared, and the FIS is ordered to disband. In June, Boudiaf is assassinated.	
1993 Violence increases, and the Armed Islamic Group (GIA) emerges as the main group behind these operations.	**1997** Hong Kong is returned to China.
1999 Abdelaziz Bouteflika is elected president. He grants amnesty to Islamic militants.	**2001** Terrorists crash planes in New York, Washington, D.C., and Pennsylvania. **2003** War in Iraq begins.
2004 President Bouteflika is reelected to a second term.	

GLOSSARY

amazigh (AH-ma-zay)
"Free man," a term Berbers call themselves

ayla (ai-la)
A small kinship unit, the members of which claim descent through the male line from a common grandfather or great-grandfather

baraka (bah-RUCK-car)
Special blessedness or grace

bin/bint (been/bee-nt)
Part of Muslim names meaning "son of" or "daughter of"

burnoose
Long hooded robe

Casbah
The old part of Algiers, from the Arabic word for a Turkish fortress

colon (koh-LOHN)
French word for "colonist"

gourbi (GOHR-be)
Rural dwelling constructed of mud and branches, stone, or clay

haik
A long piece of cloth that is draped over the body to hide the lower part of the face and cover the clothes underneath

hajj
Pilgrimage to Mecca, required of every Muslim with adequate means

Maghrib
Arabic for "west," the name geopolitically refers to a region of northern Africa including Morocco, Algeria, Tunisia, Libya, Western Sahara, and sometimes Mauritania

marabout (MARE-rah-ba-out)
Holy man

meddahas (MAD-DAH-huss)
Female poets and singers who sang Arabic love poetry

rai (rye)
A popular and traditional music indigenous to Algeria

sebkhas (SUB-kahs)
Salt marshes

shahadah (SHAR-HAR-dah)
The testimony repeated by Muslims, "There is no god but God (Allah), and Muhammad is his Prophet."

shatt (sh-UT)
Shallow salt marsh

souk
Market

tifinagh (TEE-fee-nay)
Ancient script used by the Tuareg. This is the only traditional writing for Berbers.

wadi (WAH-dee)
Dry streambed found in the Sahara that was formed during earlier wet periods

FURTHER INFORMATION

BOOKS

Ashworth, Sue. *Desserts and Sweets from Around the World*. Chicago, IL: Heinemann Library, 2004.

Camus, Albert. *Summer in Algiers*. London: Penguin, 2005.

Djebar, Assia. *The Tongue's Blood Does Not Run Dry*. New York: Seven Stories Press, 2006.

Fromentine, Eugene. *Between Sea and Sahara: An Orientalist Adventure*. New York: Tauris Parke Paperbacks: Distributed in the United States by Palgrave Macmillan, 2004.

Habeeb, William Mark. *Algeria*. Singapore: Times Editions, 2004.

Joffe, E. George H. *Algeria: The Failed Revolution*. London: Routledge, 2003.

Whitehead, Kim. *Islamic Fundamentalism*. Broomall, PA: Mason Crest Publishers, 2004.

WEB SITES

Algeria Country Analysis Brief. www.eia.doe.gov/emeu/cabs/algeria.html

Algeria.com. www.algeria.com

Arab.Net: Algeria. www.arab.net/algeria/index.html

BBC News—Country Profile: Algeria. http://news.bbc.co.uk/1/hi/world/middle_east/country_profiles/790556.stm

Central Intelligence Agency World Factbook (select Algeria from country list). www.cia.gov/library/publications/the-world-factbook/index.html

The Encyclopedia of the Orient: Algeria. http://lexicorient.com/e.o/algeria.htm

Lonely Planet WorldGuide: Algeria. www.lonelyplanet.com/worldguide/destinations/africa/algeria

FILMS

Alienations. Eurozoom, 2004.

Barakat! Pierre Grise Distribution, 2006.

The Battle of Algiers. Directed by Gillo Pontecorvo. Criterion Collection, 2004.

Desert Rose. Les Film Singuliers, 1988.

A Female Cabby in Sidi Bel-Abbes. First Run/Icarus Films, 2001.

MUSIC

Algeria: Andalusian Music from Algiers. Al-Djazaïriya al-Mossiliya. Institut du monde arabe: Harmonia Mundi, 2000.

Algeria: Troubadour from Constantine/ Tree Modes. Cheikh Salah. Buda Musique. 1998.

Honeysuckle. Souad Massi. Wrasse Records. 2005.

The Rough Guide to Rai. Cheb Khaled et al. World Music Network. 2002.

Sound of Folk Music: Algeria. Various artists. Zyx Sounds of. 2005.

BIBLIOGRAPHY

Ageron, Charles R. and Michael Brett. *Modern Algeria: A History from 1830 to the Present.* Lawrenceville, NJ: Africa World Press, 1990.

Camus, Albert. *The Stranger.* New York: Vintage, 1989.

Charrad, Mounira A. *States and Women's Rights: The Making of Postcolonial Tunisia, Algeria, and Morocco.* Berkeley, CA: University of California Press, 2002.

Djebar, Assia, translated by Marjolijn De Jager. *Women of Algiers in Their Apartment.* Charlottesville, VA: University Press of Virginia, 1992.

Lazreg, Marnia. *The Eloquence of Silence: Algerian Women in Question.* New York: Routledge, 1994.

Metz, Helen Chapin. *Algeria: A Country Study.* Washington, D.C.: Library of Congress, 1995.

Ruedy, John. *Modern Algeria: The Origins and Development of a Nation.* 2nd ed. Bloomington, IN: Indiana University Press, 2005.

Schade-Poulsen, Marc. *Men and Popular Music in Algeria.* Austin, TX: University of Texas Press, 1999.

Silverstein, Paul A. *Algeria in France: Transpolitics, Race and Nation.* Bloomington, IN: Indiana University Press, 2004.

Algeria Daily. www.algeriadaily.com

A Country Study: Algeria. http://lcweb2.loc.gov/frd/cs/dztoc.html

Maghrebia: The News and Views of the Maghreb. www.maghrebia.com/cocoon/awi/xhtml1/en_GB/homepage/default

U.S. Department of State: Algeria. www.state.gov/r/pa/ei/bgn/8005.htm

INDEX